Savoy | The Restoration

Siobhán Doran

DEWI LEWIS PUBLISHING

Savoy | The Restoration

FOREWORD

There is a small collection of hotels throughout the world that are truly legendary; icons that stand the test of time and hold a special place in people's memories. We at Fairmont Hotels & Resorts are honoured to count a number of these distinctive landmarks in our portfolio and take our role as stewards of these grand hotels very seriously.

Reopening The Savoy in October 2010, following one of London's most ambitious restoration programmes, was a true achievement and a defining moment for Fairmont. So many people worked tirelessly on the project to ensure each and every detail was just right and in step with the hotel's unrivalled reputation.

Making certain that the property reflected the essence of the hotel – what people love and remember – while also incorporating the innovations and amenities expected by today's traveller, was a delicate balance.

Over the past 100 years we have gained a reputation for our thoughtful restorations of properties such as The Plaza in New York, The Fairmont San Francisco, Canada's Fairmont Banff Springs and The Fairmont Peace Hotel in Shanghai. We appreciate the historical stake these hotels have in their communities and know many generations have passed through our doors, sharing experiences. Such properties cannot be manufactured; they are authentic, dynamic and represent many things to many people.

The restoration of The Savoy is an amazing story, as told both in pictures and words on the following pages. Thousands of artisans, craftsmen and craftswomen worked to create a new version of a beloved classic, meticulous in their efforts.

Of course, in the end, it is our guests and their experiences that help transform a hotel into an icon. We look forward to welcoming you to The Savoy and hope you have an opportunity to create many more memories at this grand hotel in the years to come.

Chris J. Cahill
President, Fairmont Hotels & Resorts
Chief Operating Officer, Fairmont
Raffles Hotels International

This informative book pays special tribute to the talent, skill, knowledge and devotion of all those who have transformed what was the fading glory of this most famous of London hotels into the dazzling splendour of The Savoy.

The ambitious restoration took almost three years. In scope and vision, there has never been a project in Britain like it. It was an undertaking that has been wonderfully captured every step of the way by the photographer Siobhán Doran. Her pictures impart, with great effect and stylistic eloquence, the elegance that embodies the spirit of The Savoy.

When this challenging project was embarked upon in 2007, the goal was to restore scrupulously the original styles of the hotel with exact authenticity, while at the same time creating new contexts and improvements that incorporate the 21st century's highest standards of comfort and service, as well as the innovations that the latest technology can provide.

With Siobhán's photographs providing a chronicle of the stages that the project went through, this book is divided into four sections. The first portrays the early days of stripping out, which, in many instances, exposed and resurrected the rich, original details that symbolized the essence of The Savoy's glorious past. The second and third sections depict the painstaking process of structural restoration and its harmonization with the new designs. The last section is devoted to the final stage of decoration and furnishing that has led to the majestic refinement exuded by The Savoy today.

I have followed with great interest and care the progress of The Savoy's restoration and feel both proud and inspired to have played a part in this remarkable achievement. The restored Savoy that now adorns the London scene is the epitome of elegance, design and refinement; an intrinsic component in the City's renown for courtliness and style. Needless to say, it was particularly gratifying to have been honoured by the presence of His Royal Highness The Prince of Wales at the reception on 2nd November 2010 to celebrate the reopening of The Savoy.

Alwaleed Bin Talal Bin Abdulaziz Alsaud
Chairman, Kingdom Holding Company

THE RESTORATION STORY

The Savoy owes its origins to the success of the famous operettas written by Gilbert and Sullivan towards the end of the 19th century. Almost from the start these had been commissioned and promoted by theatre manager and impresario Richard D'Oyly Carte. After a string of hits, D'Oyly Carte built the Savoy Theatre: modern and well-equipped with the latest electric lighting, it was designed especially to stage Gilbert and Sullivan productions.

What came to be known as the Savoy Operas were also taken by D'Oyly Carte across the Atlantic, which meant staying in some of the very newest and best hotels America had to offer. These impressed him so much with their luxury and technology that he decided to build his own back in London.

Located on the River Thames adjacent to his theatre, the new hotel took five years to build and opened on August 6, 1889. As the first true luxury hotel in London, The Savoy set completely new standards. It was the first to be lit by electricity. It had the first electric lifts, known as 'ascending rooms'. Guestrooms were connected by speaking tube to the valet, maid and floor waiter – and to other parts of the hotel, including the American Bar. Later, The Savoy became the first hotel to provide rooms with private bathrooms; these 'Savoy bathrooms' became famous for their cascading showers and quick-filling baths.

The style of the place was typically Edwardian and served London's high society at the turn of the century with all the flair and flamboyance of the times. By 1904 the hotel was such a hit that new blocks on the Strand were added. These were designed by the architect Thomas Collcutt, who had also been responsible for London's Palace Theatre and Wigmore Hall.

The last piece of The Savoy's unique stylistic character was put into place when Art Deco was introduced in the late 1920s and 30s. Sir Howard Robertson, who went on to earn a reputation for his work on the United Nations Building in New York and the Shell Centre in London, was appointed to remodel The Savoy's courtyard. Using stainless steel, which was only invented in 1928, a polished beam replaced the old flying arch spanning the roadway leading from the Strand. The adjoining Savoy Theatre and the façade of Savoy Court were also redesigned to harmonize with Robertson's elegant Art Deco handiwork. Inside, rooms and public areas were remodelled in the new style.

So this was the great legacy that challenged The Savoy in the 21st century – one of defining design styles and innovation, outstanding luxury, character and a unique role played out for more than a hundred years as a cornerstone of London high life.

But by the end of the 20th century, the building had really begun to show its age. There had been a series of piecemeal upgrades and improvements but the very fabric now required fundamental restoration. In 2005, The Savoy was purchased by HRH Prince Alwaleed Bin Talal Bin Abdulaziz Alsaud who also owns other landmark hotels around the world, including George V Paris, The Plaza New York and Raffles Singapore. Prince Alwaleed was the driving force behind the decision to temporarily close The Savoy in December 2007 for the first time in its 118-year history. This would see The Savoy relaunched in 2010 with all the flair and opulence of old.

To help with such a great task, people were needed who had an intimate knowledge of what The Savoy stood for and had achieved and who had the imagination and skill that could translate the old Savoy to 21st century standards. Thus the best possible help was enlisted from specialists around the world.

First came the architects and designers who would provide insights of what was possible in the fabric of the building. Leading this team with regard to rethinking the interior design was Pierre-Yves Rochon, well-known around the world for his luxury hospitality interior environments such as George V Paris, the Four Seasons in Florence and Hôtel Hermitage in Monaco. He has also worked for some of the world's >

> most innovative chefs, including Joel Robuchon, Alain Ducasse and Paul Bocuse.

The history and spirit of the hotel were at the forefront of Rochon's process, while creating new spaces and bringing a new vitality and freshness to the interiors. The overall design effort was realized with the help of Reardon Smith Architects and contractors The Chorus Group.

For the best part of three years, a huge team of highly skilled designers, architects, engineers, artisans and builders, worked painstakingly on restoring and recreating the true spirit of The Savoy. What has emerged is a triumphant blending of The Savoy's character built up over more than a century. The design combines The Savoy's famous two aesthetics – the Edwardian style of the original buildings and Art Deco that was introduced in the late 1920s and 30s.

The work began with the stabilisation of the river façade where steel replaced the masonry structure, allowing the riverside frontage to be redesigned and provide more space for guestrooms. Also on this side of the building the *porte cochère* was refurbished and all the windows replaced to an authentic design. Meanwhile on the Strand side, the entrance was given a new granite forecourt, a Lalique crystal fountain and a restored Art Deco roof.

Characteristic features and places, as well as some new elements and spaces, have emerged from the restorations. The Front Hall has been opened up with the removal of the reception desk, while marble columns and the sylvan frieze have been renovated along with the mahogany panelling. The Thames Foyer has become the heart of the hotel again, with its new winter garden gazebo beneath a spectacular glass cupola. Adjoining it is Savoy Tea, a new bijou tea store and patisserie which evokes a sense of the classic arcade shops of Piccadilly.

New life has been breathed into The Savoy's restaurants and bars which have always played such a big part in its reputation. The River Restaurant, made famous by chef Auguste Escoffier after the hotel first opened, is reborn with an Art Deco-inspired design and modern French menu. The Savoy Grill is also back with its original seating plan. Under the management of Gordon Ramsay, it features the Grill menu classics which made its name, some given a modern twist.

The American Bar, one of the very first cocktail bars in London, is thoroughly restored but essentially looks unchanged. By contrast the Beaufort Bar is brand new, focusing on champagne, cocktails and cabaret. On the spot where the Savoy Bands once entertained revellers and dancing guests, the bar's Art Deco-inspired

scheme of jet-black and burnished gold now makes a spectacular setting for the return of cabaret to London.

On the fifth floor, The Savoy's new Royal Suite redefines imperial splendour, with its eight rooms stretching the length of the building overlooking the Thames, each offering the famous views as painted by Monet. Other riverside suites have also been reconfigured to enhance their views of the Thames, a signature feature of the hotel. The Art Deco rooms have been faithfully restored and the Edwardian rooms refurbished.

The Savoy has always been a hub of London society. All the event and meeting rooms, including the great Lancaster Ballroom and the famous Art Deco meeting rooms named after Gilbert and Sullivan operettas, have been restored. The hotel's great traditions and idiosyncrasies are also preserved: Savoy Court remains the only street in Britain where vehicles are required to drive on the right.

The Savoy finally opened its doors again on '10.10.10'. The abiding impression is one of something familiar yet at once entirely new and splendid. The approval has been unanimous; the applause enthusiastic.

CHAPTER ONE | EXPOSING ORIGINAL DETAIL

5TH FLOOR RIVER VIEW SUITES | DECEMBER 2007

Initially, I set to work during the Savoy Sale, the December 2007 auction staged by Bonhams at the hotel. I decided to photograph the nine River View Suites stretching across the fifth floor during the two-day duration of this event. It was the only time that I could shoot these rooms, because prior to the auction they were fully booked. The Savoy's fifth floor is its centre. Every room on that level has a spectacular river view offering a unique perspective. In each room, the desk and chair – which I repositioned to face the window – represented, to me, the people who have passed through the hotel during its 118-year history. The furniture was affixed with Bonhams' auction tags, which signifies the present, while the view – displaying the River Thames, the Royal Festival Hall and the London Eye – grounds each image, establishing a sense of the hotel's London presence and also symbolizing its future. So the sequence ponders The Savoy's past and contemplates what is yet to come.

Beaufort Bar | The Winter Garden

River View Guestrooms | A Touch of Elegance

CHAPTER TWO | STRUCTURAL RESTORATION

Once the strip-out progressed to the bare bones, the enormity of the job was unveiled. The replacement of the original masonry structure with steel at the south side of the building left the river rooms filled with a maze of scaffolding. As the construction team began to rebuild the core of the building, I was inspired to capture the new markings and traces left by this structural work. I was aware that these observations would soon be covered over with new layers of finishes, only to reappear in years to come, should future generations find themselves restoring The Savoy once again – perhaps becoming the new smiling ghosts of the Savoy's past?

The photographs *River Suite – 7th floor* (page 51) encapsulates the mood of that moment in time – one of endurance, strength and change. Although poised at a construction stage of great significance, soon the engineers' work would be complete and a blank canvas would be left for the craftspeople to embellish.

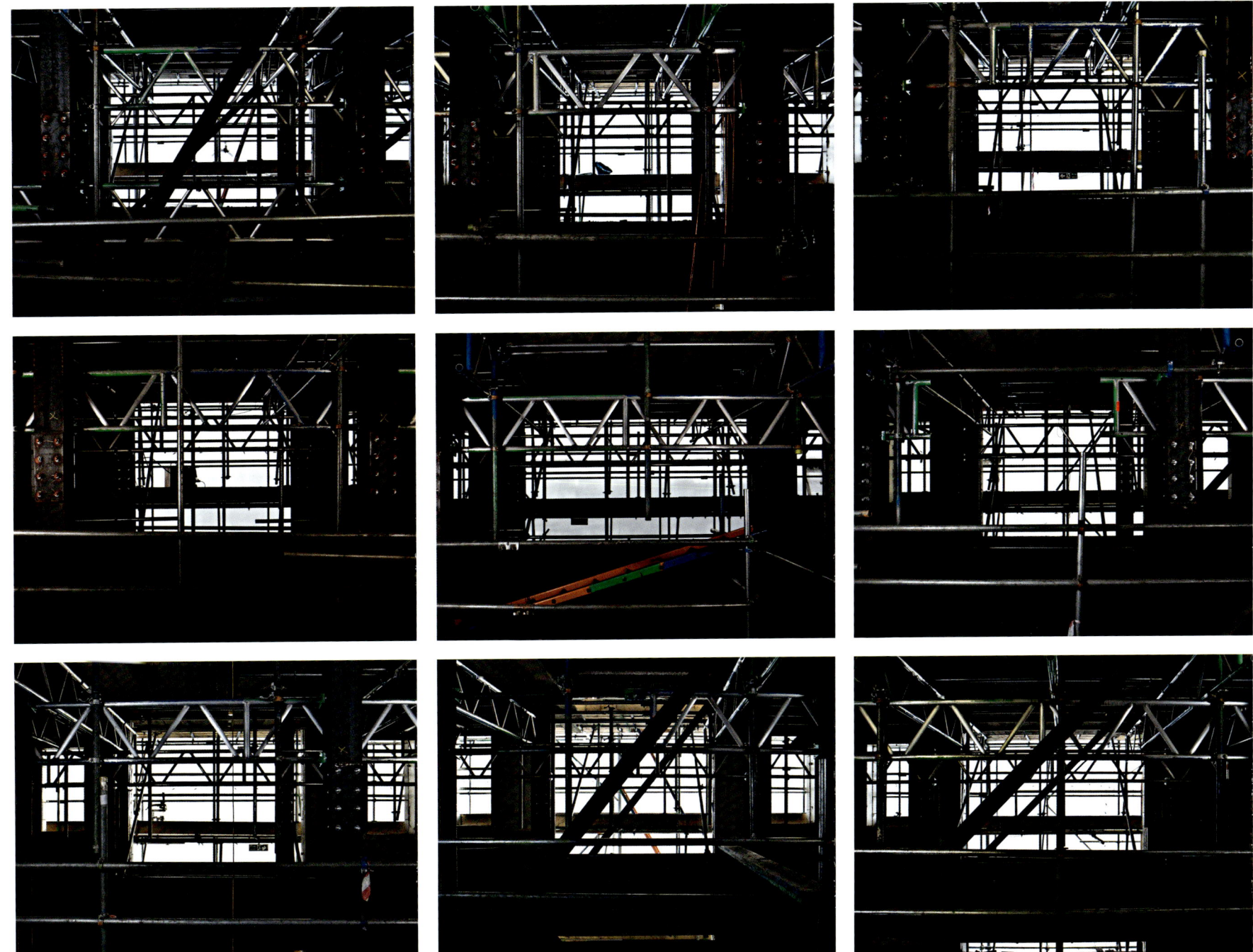

Upper Thames Foyer | Semi-Secret Vantage Point

Thames Foyer | Natural Light

RIVER VIEW | CITY ILLUMINATIONS

Chapter Three | The New Design

5TH FLOOR ROYAL SUITE | AUGUST 2009

With the completion of the structural work and the removal of the internal scaffolding, natural light returned to the interior spaces. The Lower Thames Foyer was glowing like a stage under its grand new dome, which was flooding the space with beautiful daylight. There was an air of optimism to the site – although still a long way from completion, the feeling of being able to see light at the end of the tunnel was unanimous. The dark days were (quite literally) over. The visibility of the new design seemed to create a furore of excitement, and the opening date was confirmed. Once this date was set the hotel swarmed with the largest amount of workers it had seen throughout the whole programme, and they worked day and night to meet their deadline.

For me, each visit at this stage of the restoration uncovered a new delight. The photograph *Royal Suite – silk-wrapped chandelier* (page 85) summed up this inspiring time as finished pieces were being installed alongside plastering and painting. Miniature 'Christo and Jeanne-Claudes' were to be seen around every corner.

Royal Suite | The Jewel in the Crown

Thames Foyer | A Royal Event

River Room Suite | An Artist's Eye View

CHAPTER FOUR | THE FINISHING TOUCHES

The days running up to the opening were frantic. Security guards were posted in all finished areas and for the first time I had to obtain a permit to enter particular zones. For the first time also, I was asked to leave the Royal Suite as there were already too many people working in unison. I left quietly, mindful of the pressure the craftspeople were under to complete on time. That same day I returned to the ground floor, approaching it at the Upper Thames Foyer. I was taken aback. The artwork and antiques had arrived and were being positioned; clusters of variously sized frames were been hung alongside overflowing cabinets of antiques – the room was alive! Almost instantly the elegance and glamour that had been temporarily obscured was uncovered, and I imagined the Foyer bustling with guests as they went about their business to the background music of the hotel's pianist in the Thames Foyer.

Lancaster Ballroom | Former Glory

Beaufort Bar | Gilded Elegance

In the past, I had been privileged to be able to photograph a derelict well-known London hotel. The images I had produced at that time excited me, as I could feel the history of the building and imagine the stories of its past.

A good friend of mine introduced me to members of The Savoy's management at the beginning of the building's major restoration, and following our first meeting in the American Bar I submitted a proposal for a collection of images to capture the progress of the works. My exhilaration at the project's potential was quickly met by emotional free fall as the proposal was rejected. However, I would say that my enthusiasm to undertake this project matched the passion and spirit with which The Savoy was to be painstakingly restored. A further proposal convinced the management, allowing me unlimited access for the duration of the project.

This work was created more by intuition than design. I had no prior connection with the hotel but had worked with buildings, both as a designer and a photographer, for many years. My background gave me an understanding of the enormity of the process that was to lie ahead, and also the scale of the opportunity. Empty, the 118-year-old hotel was charged with possibilities.

At the beginning of the project I was attempting to establish a direction for my photography, but I soon realised that I needed to trust my instincts and capture what struck me, what made an impact. On taking the first set of nine River View Suites photographs, I felt I had found a focus; I knew I would return to these rooms repeatedly. This seemed ironic because although I was not sure of the direction for the entire body of work, I knew that this set of nine photographs was important.

Whilst editing the final work, after almost 100 visits to the hotel, I became aware that although I had consciously returned to these fifth floor River View Suites throughout the project, I had also unconsciously revisited particular areas elsewhere in the building over and over.

My intuition had led me to a concept: that of returning, revisiting, relooking at and remaking the same images. The difference here, however, was that I had not kept to a prescribed format, as I had with the River View Suites. Perhaps this approach also unconsciously reflects the many views and insights that the hotel's customers observe – depending on the season in which they visit, the length of their stay, the areas that they frequent and whether it is their first visit or, like mine, one of many.

Siobhán Doran
Hertfordshire, July 2011

THE TEAM

It is a fitting tribute to every individual who worked on this project that a book should be published to recognize and reward their achievements. My gratitude goes to Fairmont Hotels & Resorts and everyone involved with The Savoy for their tremendous support and encouragement throughout the restoration and construction period. Due to the dedication of the professional team and the hard work and support of our loyal subcontractors, we have been able to deliver a building that is spectacularly constructed and beautifully finished.

My admiration and sincere thanks go to my staff at Chorus Group for their unwavering commitment to perfection and the sleepless nights they endured, which are so quickly forgotten. I am honoured that Byrne Group, and in particular Chorus, have been entrusted with delivering the most ambitious and elaborate restoration of a British hotel in history.

Patsy Byrne
CEO, Byrne Group plc

N ABAH ✦ G ABBOTT ✦ M ABDELATY ✦ M ABDIRAZAK ✦ L ABDULLAHI ✦ K ABRAHAM ✦ D ABRAHAMS ✦ C ABRAHAMS ✦ V ACATRINEI ✦ T ACDRIDGE ✦ L ACRAMAN ✦ B ACTON ✦ A ADALUMO ✦ N ADAMS ✦ D ADAWAY ✦ I ADDAI-DWQMOTT ✦ I ADEBARI ✦ M ADEKOLA ✦ A ADELEKE ✦ A ADEMOLA ✦ ADENIYI ✦ O ADEROUNMU ✦ O ADEWALE ✦ O ADEYANJU ✦ H ADI ✦ F ADJEI ✦ A ADOMENAS ✦ U ADRIAN ✦ O ADRIAN ✦ J ADRIAN-MIHAI ✦ A ADRIAN-STELIAN ✦ D ADU ✦ F ADU ✦ D ADU ✦ M ADZHILARSKI ✦ K AGBOKA ✦ R AGNEW ✦ R AGORDZO ✦ O AGUELE ✦ E AGYEI ✦ B AHMED ✦ S AHMET ✦ T AHMET ✦ J AIDOO ✦ T AIJAZ ✦ D AILIOAEI ✦ J AIREY ✦ A AJAYI ✦ M AJAYI ✦ A AKHUETIEMEN ✦ B AKINBOBOLA ✦ E AKINDE ✦ O AKINSANYA ✦ A ALABI ✦ S ALAO ✦ K ALAYANDE ✦ M ALBERT ✦ S ALBON ✦ A ALDIS ✦ S ALDIS ✦ D ALDRED ✦ M ALDRICH ✦ P ALEXA ✦ D ALEXANDER ✦ J ALEXANDER ✦ A ALEXANDER ✦ D ALEXANDER ✦ I ALEXANDRU ✦ M ALEXANDRU ✦ P ALEXANDRU ✦ I ALI ✦ M ALI ✦ L ALIKOLLAR ✦ O ALIMA ✦ A ALINGBADE ✦ L ALLA ✦ L ALLARD ✦ D ALLARO ✦ B ALLEN ✦ D ALLEN ✦ D ALLEN ✦ G ALLEN ✦ J ALLEN ✦ H ALLEN ✦ P ALLEN ✦ D ALLSOP ✦ J ALSTON ✦ P AMADI ✦ G AMANKWAH ✦ A AMARIEI ✦ N AMBER ✦ A AMBROSIO ✦ N AMEV ✦ G AMOAKOH ✦ I ANANE ✦ G ANDAI ✦ L ANDEREYA ✦ R ANDERSON ✦ C ANDERSON ✦ R ANDERSON ✦ J ANDERSON ✦ M ANDERSON ✦ F ANDONE ✦ V ANDREWS ✦ S ANDREWS ✦ B ANDREWS ✦ A ANDRIJAITIS ✦ S ANDZIUS ✦ T ANGRAVE ✦ A ANITA ✦ J ANREP ✦ M ANTAL ✦ A ANTONIO ✦ G APARNAGIU ✦ M APETROAEI ✦ S APOSTOLOV ✦ K APPIAH ✦ B ARDESSLAM ✦ J ARGENT ✦ S ARGENT ✦ E ARLAUSKAS ✦ G ARMSTRONG ✦ C ARNAUTU ✦ B ARNOLD ✦ L ARNOLD ✦ P ARNOULD ✦ O ARO ✦ E AROWOSAFE ✦ C ARROWSMITH ✦ M ARTHUR ✦ F ARTHUR ✦ P ARTHUR ✦ G ARTICO ✦ R ASANTE ✦ J ASBRIDGE ✦ J ASHAOLU ✦ K ASHCROFT ✦ M ASHER ✦ K ASIAMAH ✦ D ASLETT ✦ M ASMUSSEN ✦ J ASTEL ✦ A ATKINS ✦ D ATKINS ✦ M ATKINS ✦ K ATKINSON ✦ L ATTERTON ✦ I ATTILA ✦ A AUGUSTINAS ✦ A AUSTEN ✦ P AUSTEN ✦ O AUSTEN ✦ N AUSTIN ✦ S AVADANEI ✦ I AVRAMUT ✦ A AYANWALE ✦ Y AYETAN ✦ A AYODESI ✦ B AYOUB ✦ J AYRES ✦ S AYRES ✦ F AZEMI ✦ M BACIU ✦ I BACRIS ✦ K BADURA ✦ D BAERNREUTHER ✦ A BAFFOUR ✦ K BAGNAL ✦ C BAGSHAW ✦ A BAILEY ✦ J BAILEY ✦ M BAILEY ✦ L BAILEY

✦ R BAINS ✦ G BAIRD ✦ A BAIRD ✦ M BAJRACHARYA ✦ S BAKALA ✦ M BALABAN ✦ D BALABANOU ✦ G BALAISIS ✦ C BALARINE ✦ V BALAS ✦ S BALCHIN ✦ E BALDAU ✦ J BALDOCK ✦ S BALDWIN ✦ A BALDWIN ✦ R BALKEVICIUS ✦ S BALL ✦ D BALOGUN ✦ V BALTRUSAITIS ✦ D BALUIKONIS ✦ B BALUSI ✦ S BAMIGBOYE ✦ R BANAHENE ✦ I BANCILA ✦ H BANGURA ✦ H BANGHAM ✦ A BANKOWSKI ✦ A BANU ✦ A BANU ✦ P BARA ✦ R BARATH ✦ A BARBER ✦ N BARBER ✦ L BARBER ✦ C BARCLAY ✦ I BARHAM ✦ D BARHAM ✦ G BARKER ✦ R BARKER ✦ G BARLETT ✦ P BARLOW ✦ P BARNARD ✦ D BARNES ✦ C BARNES ✦ S BARNES ✦ P BARNETT ✦ L BARNUSCA ✦ O BARON ✦ J BARR ✦ P BARRETT ✦ S BARRETT ✦ G BARRETT ✦ E BARRETT ✦ C BARRETT ✦ A BARRETT ✦ B BARTHOLOMEW ✦ B BARTHOLOMEW ✦ D BARTLAM ✦ M BARTMANOWICZ ✦ A BARTNIK ✦ W BARZYCKI ✦ B BASILE ✦ G BASOULU ✦ L BASTONS ✦ J BATEMAN ✦ A BATES ✦ P BATT ✦ A BATU ✦ M BAXTER ✦ P BAYLISS ✦ S BAYOUMY ✦ N BEARD ✦ A BEARD ✦ J BEASLEY ✦ D BEATSON ✦ A BEATTIE ✦ N BECHTEL ✦ G BECK ✦ A BECKLET ✦ T BECKWITH ✦ A BEDFORD ✦ R BEECH ✦ G BEEDLE ✦ T BEER ✦ J BEETON ✦ M BEJENARU ✦ A BELCEANU ✦ A BELCIUG ✦ S BELENSKI ✦ J BELL ✦ M BELL ✦ S BELL ✦ N BENAINRA ✦ R BENDORAITIS ✦ T BENEDIC ✦ V BENIULIS ✦ A BENNETT ✦ A BENNETT ✦ C BENNETT ✦ J BENNETT ✦ J BENNETT ✦ S BENNETT ✦ P BENNING ✦ T BENSON ✦ G BERISHA ✦ A BERISHA ✦ N BERKO ✦ V BERKUS ✦ L BERRY ✦ J BERRY ✦ D BERRY ✦ S BERTASIUS ✦ L BETHAZ ✦ M BEVAN ✦ R BIDDLE ✦ M BIDVAS ✦ R BIDWELL ✦ L BIKINAS ✦ B BIN SUKAM ✦ HRH PRINCE ALWALEED BIN TALAL BIN ABDULAZIZ AL SAUD ✦ P BINDING ✦ E BINNS ✦ S BIRD ✦ J BISHOP ✦ R BISHOP ✦ C BISOC ✦ S BLACK ✦ D BLACKBURN ✦ J BLACKBURN ✦ A BLACKMAN ✦ W BLAIK ✦ N BLAKE ✦ R BLAND ✦ B BLASZIZAK ✦ J BLENNERHASSETT ✦ J BLEWITT ✦ I BLONDELL ✦ Z BLONSKI ✦ R BOARDMAN ✦ K BOATENG ✦ P BOCA ✦ V BOCHEV ✦ G BODOC ✦ I BODOC ✦ S BODOCAN ✦ M BOGACKI ✦ T BOGDAN ✦ A BOGOVENKO ✦ V BOIAN ✦ C BOICU ✦ L BOLAND ✦ M BOLDAV ✦ D BOLLAND ✦ M BOLOCAN ✦ R BOLTON ✦ R BONAR ✦ E BONDORET ✦ K BONEV ✦ A BONNER ✦ J BOON ✦ K BOON ✦ A BOOTH ✦ T BOOTHE ✦ P BOOTLE ✦ A BORDUN ✦ M BORISOV ✦ H BORLAND ✦ D BOROS ✦ A BOROTA ✦ E BOSCHE ✦ S BOSEV ✦ T BOSEV ✦ P BOSHELL ✦ D BOSHOFF ✦ K BOSWELL ✦ T BOUARU ✦ P BOVILL ✦ S BOWAS ✦ M BOWEN ✦ M BOWERS ✦ B BOWLES ✦ B BOXALL ✦ D BOYLAN ✦ C BOYLE ✦ C BOYLE ✦ D BOZHKOV ✦ M BRADBURY ✦ L BRADLY ✦ A BRAGG ✦ A BRAHMBHATT ✦ N BRAMBLEY ✦ N BRAN ✦ C BRANT ✦ A BRAY ✦ J BRAY ✦ D BREADMAN ✦ B BREAZU ✦ D BRETON ✦ S BRETT ✦ A BREWER ✦ J BREWER ✦ P BREWERTON ✦ D BREWSTER ✦ P BRIGGS ✦ J BRIGHT ✦ H BRIMBLE ✦ G BRISCOE ✦ S BRITNELL ✦ W BRITS ✦ M BROCK ✦ C BRODERICK ✦ T BROJEWSKI ✦ W BROJEWSKI ✦ R BROOK ✦ B BROOKS ✦ A BROOMFIELD ✦ A BROOMHEAD ✦ B BROWN ✦ G BROWN ✦ K BROWN ✦ K BROWN ✦ L BROWN ✦ L BROWN ✦ M BROWN ✦ S BROWN ✦ W BROWN ✦ K BROWNLIE ✦ P BRUNS ✦ D BRYAN ✦ M BRYAN ✦ J BUCKLAND ✦ M BUCKMAN ✦ S BUDD ✦ I BUDEANU ✦ G BUDI ✦ J BULL ✦ J BULLION ✦ D BULMAN ✦ D BUNIAK ✦ M BUNN ✦ D BUOZINIS ✦ A BURCH ✦ R BURCHELL ✦ A BURCIU ✦ D BURDALSKI ✦ N BURDON ✦ N BURDUCEA ✦ S BURFIELD ✦ S BURGIN ✦ S BURKE ✦ J BURLACU ✦ R BURNS ✦ S BURNSIDE ✦ D BURRIDGE ✦ M BURT ✦ P BURT ✦ G BURT ✦ T BURTENSHAW ✦ J BURTON ✦ M BUSCHI ✦ C BUSH ✦ K BUSH ✦ R BUSH ✦ R BUSTAN ✦ G BUTCHER ✦ P BUTCHER ✦ P BUTCHER ✦ W BUTCHER ✦ M BUTKOVIC ✦ D BUTLER ✦ P BUTLER ✦ C BYRNE ✦ J BYRNE ✦ J BYRNE ✦ M BYRNE ✦ N BYRNE ✦ P BYRNE ✦ S BYRNE ✦ T BYRNE ✦ W BYRNE ✦ J CADDOCK ✦ C CADLE ✦ M CAHILL ✦ P CAIL ✦ D CAINS ✦ S CAIRNS ✦ D CAKEBREAD ✦ B CAKIAI ✦ P CALLAGHAN ✦ M CALLEJA ✦ D CAMBRELL ✦ D CAMERON ✦ A CAMPBELL ✦ D CAMPBELL ✦ G CAMPBELL ✦ I CAMPBELL ✦ J CAMPBELL ✦ N CAMPBELL ✦ P CAMPBELL ✦ R CAMPBELL ✦ S CAMPBELL ✦ T CAMPBELL ✦ T CAMPBELL ✦ J CANEY ✦ J CANHAM ✦ T CANNING ✦ I CAPATINA ✦ R CAPLIN ✦ I CAPON ✦ J CAPPER ✦ C CAPRAR ✦ P CARD ✦ M CARE ✦ K CAREY ✦ S CARLEY ✦ F CARLOS DE MORAIS ✦ M CARLSSON ✦ S CARNEY ✦ A CARPENTER ✦ R CARPENTER ✦ M CARPENTER ✦ D CARR ✦ M CARR ✦ C CARRAN ✦ S CARRINGTON ✦ C CARTER ✦ J CARTER ✦ P CARTER ✦ S CARTER ✦ J CARVALHO ✦ V CASPAO ✦ R CASPER ✦ P CASSETTARI ✦ M CASSIDY ✦ D CASSINI-ORELLECA ✦ D CATALIN ✦ V CAVALCIUC ✦ J CAWLEY ✦ L CAWSTON ✦ D CAZAH ✦ I CECH ✦ I CEPREAGA ✦ A CERNIAUSKAS ✦ S CEZAR ✦ R CHALK ✦ L CHALKLIN ✦ P CHALMERS ✦ E CHAMBERLAIN ✦ B CHAMBERS ✦ D CHAMBERS ✦ R CHAMPLIN ✦ C CHANCE ✦ L CHANDLER ✦ L CHANDLER ✦ D CHAPPELL ✦ M CHAPPLE ✦ T CHARANIA ✦ A CHARLES ✦ B CHARLES ✦ G CHARLES ✦ C CHARLIE ✦ F CHARRVA ✦ D CHATFIELD ✦ A CHAVDA ✦ T CHEESEMAN ✦ A CHELBA ✦ D CHELWYND ✦ A CHENG ✦ J CHESHAM ✦ S CHESTERMAN ✦ S CHEYNE ✦ A CHEUNG ✦ B CHIKOVANI ✦ P CHILD ✦ A CHINDRIS ✦ E CHINSMAN ✦ V CHIOGO ✦ S CHIPPERFIELD ✦ I CHIRIAC ✦ I CHISHOLM ✦ D CHITTOCK ✦ L CHITU ✦ M CHOGUGUDZA ✦ K CHOROMARISHI ✦ J CHRISTENSEN ✦ J CHRISTIAN ✦ N CHRISTIAN ✦ D CHRISTOPHER ✦ P CHRUSCINSKI ✦ M CHUBBOCK ✦ M CHUKWU ✦ V CHUVAROVA ✦ N CICIC ✦ H CIFTCI ✦ S CINI ✦ R CIORTEA ✦ P CIPRIAN ✦ S CIPRIAN ✦ F CIPRIAN ✦ I CIRMACI ✦ M CIRMACI ✦ R CIURARU ✦ A CIUREA ✦ M CIZMAR ✦ J CLAIRMONTE ✦ R CLAREE-DIXON ✦ A CLARK ✦ B CLARK ✦ D CLARK ✦ L CLARK ✦ C CLARKE ✦ G CLARKE ✦ J CLARKE ✦ K CLARKE ✦ L CLARKE ✦ L CLARKE ✦ R CLARKE ✦ S CLARKE ✦ W CLARKE ✦ M CLAUDOMIR ✦ S CLAWSON ✦ D CLAYDEN ✦ B CLAYTON ✦ J CLEAR ✦ M CLEMENTS ✦ D CLIFFORD ✦ A CLIMPSON ✦ A CLIMPTON ✦ B CLOETE ✦ J CLOUD ✦ T CLOUGH ✦ A COATES ✦ S COBB ✦ G COBUZ ✦ T COCKCROFT ✦ N COCKINGS ✦ C COE ✦ J COFFEY ✦ J COFFEY ✦ R COJOCARU ✦ C COJOCARU ✦ L COKER ✦ A COLE ✦ N COLE ✦ K COLEMAN ✦ M COLEY ✦ K COLLINS ✦ R COLLINS ✦ S COLLINS ✦ F COMISESCU ✦ S COMMINS ✦ A COMPA ✦ J COMPSON ✦ L COMPTON ✦ K CONLAY ✦ S CONLON ✦ J CONNELLY ✦ R CONNOLLY ✦ A CONNOR ✦ B CONROY ✦ A CONSTANTIN ✦ D CONSTANTIN ✦ T CONSTANTINIDES ✦ C COOK ✦ R COOK ✦ D COOKE ✦ R COOKE ✦ J COOMBS ✦ C COOPER ✦ D COOPER ✦ J COOPER ✦ J COOPER ✦ P COOPER ✦ S COOPER ✦ A COPE ✦ J COPPCOCK ✦ K CORBETT ✦ G CORBETT ✦ P CORDINGLEY ✦ S CORKHILL ✦ K CORMACK ✦ J CORNEL-ERIMIA ✦ G CORNFORD ✦ G CORNWELL ✦ P CORRIGAN ✦ P CORRIGAN ✦ S COSIS ✦ R COSSON ✦ D COSTA ✦ M COSTACHE ✦ I COSTEA ✦ F COSTIN ✦ J COTIER ✦ S COTTAM ✦ K COTTEE ✦ A COTTLE ✦ M COTTON ✦ P COTTRELL ✦ M COULTON ✦ J COURTNEY ✦ N COUSIN ✦ N COUSIN ✦ S COUSIN ✦ K COUZENS ✦ J COWLEY ✦ D COWLEY-COULTON ✦ A COX ✦ D COX ✦ D COX ✦ C COZAC ✦ C COZMA ✦ D CRACIUN ✦ S CRADDOCK ✦ M CRAFT ✦ I CRAGG ✦ M CRAIG ✦ F CRATHERN ✦ M CRAWFORD ✦ P CRAWFORD ✦ B CRAWLEY ✦ I CREANGA ✦ P CREANGA ✦ F CREANGA ✦ S CREGEEN ✦ L CRESTIANI ✦ L CRICKMAR ✦ M CRILLY ✦ L CRINGANU ✦ A CRIPPS ✦ J CRISPINO ✦ N CRISTINEL ✦ T CROFT ✦ T CRONK ✦ G CROSS ✦ J CROSS ✦ K CROWLEY ✦ T CRUMLISH ✦ R CUDLIPP ✦ M CULHAM ✦ C CULLANE ✦ P CULLEN ✦ G CULLEN ✦ T CULLEN ✦ R CURBISON ✦ J CURD ✦ N CURD ✦ P CURRAN ✦ T CURSON ✦ P CURTIS ✦ B CURTIS ✦ P CZAJKOWSKI ✦ D CZAPOR ✦ M CZARNIECKI ✦ Z CZASA ✦ T CZECZOT ✦ DD COSTA ✦ C DA SILVA ✦ T DA SILVA ✦ S DACEY ✦ J DADD ✦ A

DAHELE ✦ A DALLING ✦ C DALTREY ✦ P DAMARIO ✦ A DAMBRAUSKAS ✦ V DAMIAN ✦ R DAN ✦ T DANCE ✦ V DANCHOV ✦ M DANDOCZI ✦ S DANDU ✦ C DANIEL ✦ U DANIEL ✦ T DANIELS ✦ T DANIELS ✦ K DANILOV ✦ K DANKWAH ✦ M DANN ✦ M DANN ✦ A DANOVSKIS ✦ S DAOUNOV ✦ P DARCY ✦ S DARCY ✦ D DARIUS ✦ E DARKO ✦ J DARKO ✦ O DARKWA ✦ C DARLINGTON ✦ H DATCU ✦ W DATE ✦ S DAVENPORT ✦ A DAVIDSON ✦ A DAVIES ✦ D DAVIES ✦ M DAVIES ✦ P DAVIES ✦ T DAVIES ✦ A DAVIS ✦ E DAVIS ✦ P DAVIS ✦ P DAVIS ✦ T DAVIS ✦ J DAVOREM ✦ S DAVY ✦ R DAWKINS ✦ O DAWODU ✦ D DAWSON ✦ M DAY ✦ J DAY ✦ J DAY ✦ J DE BEER ✦ J DE CAMPI ✦ M DE CAMPI ✦ P DE PODESTA ✦ P DE WIT ✦ F DEAC ✦ R DEACON ✦ P DEADMAN ✦ C DEAN ✦ A DEANS ✦ J DEASY ✦ M DEJU ✦ R DELL ✦ J DENEHAN ✦ M DERMILOV ✦ N DESAI ✦ T DESBROW ✦ C DEWSEM ✦ O DEYNEHA ✦ S DIAS ✦ S DICHEV ✦ S DIDA ✦ S DIGBY ✦ S DIL ✦ M DILLON ✦ L DILWORTH ✦ D DILWORTH ✦ N DIMUNA ✦ G DINE ✦ I DINESCU ✦ V DINESCU ✦ K DINKOV ✦ C DINNING ✦ J DITCHFIELD ✦ J DIVERS ✦ C DIX ✦ A DIXON ✦ G DIXON ✦ S DIXON ✦ N DMITRICENKO ✦ G DOBOS ✦ R DOBRAUSKAS ✦ D DOBRE ✦ S DOBROVOLSKIS ✦ P DOBSON ✦ S DOHERTY ✦ A DOHERTY ✦ T DOHOV ✦ P DOKTOV ✦ S DOLAN ✦ D DOLEA ✦ K DOM ✦ N DOMMETT ✦ D DONCA ✦ Y DONEVSKI ✦ P DONNIGAN ✦ J DONOVAN ✦ G DONU ✦ N DOOGAN ✦ J DOONAN ✦ F DORALI ✦ S DORAN ✦ S DORAN ✦ G DORMAND ✦ T DORNELLY ✦ S DOUBELL ✦ A DOUBLE ✦ N DOUGHERTY ✦ J DOW ✦ W DOWARRIS ✦ B DOWD ✦ T DOWLE ✦ G DOWLING ✦ O DOWNER ✦ A DOWNES ✦ C DOWNS ✦ G DOYLE ✦ L DRAGANOIS ✦ M DRAGANOIU ✦ R DRAGOI ✦ F DRAGOMIR ✦ I DRAGOMIR ✦ V DRAGOMIR ✦ F DRAGOMIR ✦ L DRAWATER ✦ P DRISCOLL ✦ K DRUMCHEV ✦ J DRYDEN ✦ A DRYDEN ✦ M DRYSDALE ✦ H DU BRUYN ✦ S DU PLESSIS ✦ F DU PREEZ ✦ S DUAH ✦ G DUBARRY ✦ P DUBRA ✦ V DUDLANSKAS ✦ T DUDLEY ✦ G DUDLEY ✦ R DUDUTA ✦ A DUFFY ✦ W DUGGAN ✦ M DUKE ✦ L DUMA ✦ M DUMITRACHE ✦ M DUMITRASCU ✦ R DUMITRU ✦ G DUMITRU ✦ I DUMITRU ✦ J DUMONT ✦ A DUNAJSKI ✦ A DUNCAN ✦ I DUNCAN ✦ P DUNCAN ✦ J DUNFORD ✦ I DUNLOP ✦ R DUNN ✦ S DUPONTET ✦ M DURA ✦ K DURBRIDGE ✦ N DURNIAN ✦ D DURRANT ✦ E DUTA ✦ G DUTA ✦ S DUTTON ✦ R DWOJAK ✦ P DYER ✦ J DYKE ✦ M DYSON ✦ P DZEHA ✦ A DZHUGDANOV ✦ M DZHURELOV ✦ L DZIATKIEWICZ ✦ D DZIEKIEWICZ ✦ G DZIUBEK ✦ J EAGLE ✦ J EARWICKER ✦ H EAST ✦ P EASTERBROOK ✦ S EASTHAM ✦ C EATON ✦ M EBRAHIMI ✦ A EBRAHIMY ✦ D EBRAHIMY ✦ N ECCLES ✦ R EDE ✦ S EDGE ✦ C EDKINS ✦ C EDWARD ✦ A EDWARDS ✦ A EDWARDS ✦ A EDWARDS ✦ B EDWARDS ✦ L EDWARDS ✦ R EDWARDS ✦ J EELES ✦ J EGGLETON ✦ F EHIOGHAE ✦ S EHOMNU ✦ J EKELEGBU ✦ T EL-GENDY ✦ L ELDRED ✦ I ELDRIDGE ✦ I ELENA ✦ I ELENA ✦ A ELIAS ✦ M ELISEI ✦ J ELLIOTT ✦ J ELLIOTT ✦ S ELLIOTT ✦ J ELLIS ✦ J ELLIS ✦ R ELLIS ✦ S ELPHICK ✦ M ELVIS ✦ B EMBER ✦ P EMBLEN ✦ T EMILIAN ✦ J EMMINES ✦ M ENE ✦ B ENGLISH ✦ P ENGLISH ✦ S ENGLISH ✦ J EOSCIEJ ✦ N EPURE ✦ A ERMAKOV ✦ A ERONDU ✦ C EUGENIU ✦ A EVANS ✦ G EVANS ✦ P EVANS ✦ R EVANS ✦ S EVANS ✦ D EVE ✦ C EVERETT ✦ R EVERITT ✦ S EVERITT ✦ T EVETT ✦ P EXON ✦ P FAGAN ✦ O FAGBOLA ✦ M FAHEY ✦ M FAIRBRASS ✦ K FAIRMAN ✦ C FAITH ✦ G FANCE ✦ R FANCE ✦ T FANCE ✦ A FARAONIO ✦ G FARMER ✦ J FARMER ✦ M FARQUHARSON ✦ N FARR ✦ L FARRANT ✦ R FARRELL ✦ R FARRELL ✦ K FARRINGTON ✦ N FARRINGTON ✦ A FASOGBON ✦ L FAULL ✦ A FAY ✦ S FAY ✦ S FEARON ✦ G FEAST ✦ S FEATHERSTONE ✦ P FEATHERSTONE ✦ R FEDDEN ✦ G FEE ✦ G FEE ✦ A FENNELL ✦ G FERARIU ✦ J FERRARI ✦ S FERREIRA ✦ J FERRY ✦ G FFRENCH ✦ L FIEDURA ✦ K FINCH ✦ M FINCH ✦ N FINCH ✦ E FINN ✦ D FIOLEK ✦ N FIONDA ✦ D FIRMIN ✦ S FIRMIN ✦ G FIRMIN ✦ R FISHER ✦ R FISHER ✦ S FISHER ✦ T FISHLOCK ✦ E FITZGERALD ✦ J FITZGERALD ✦ J FITZPATRICK ✦ H FITZPATRICK ✦ T FITZSIMMONS ✦ K FLAHERTY ✦ C FLAIN ✦ D FLAIN ✦ O FLAVIU ✦ P FLAVIUS ARNOLD ✦ D FLECKENSTEIN ✦ M FLECTHER ✦ M FLEMING ✦ P FLEMMING ✦ L FLOOD ✦ L FLORIN ✦ A FLORIN-TONI ✦ J FLYNN ✦ D FLYNN ✦ D FLYNN ✦ I FOFANA ✦ C FOLEY ✦ P FOLTIN ✦ V FOMENKO ✦ J FONSECA ✦ Z FORD ✦ K FORDE ✦ P FORDHAM ✦ L FOREMAN ✦ P FORKES ✦ A FORREST ✦ G FORSTER ✦ A FORSYTH ✦ P FORTUNE ✦ A FOSTER ✦ M FOSTER ✦ R FOSTER ✦ D FOSTER ✦ N FOSTER ✦ C FOSTER ✦ P FOX ✦ J FOX ✦ N FOX ✦ D FRANCE ✦ J FRANCES ✦ I FRANCIS ✦ F FRANCO ✦ J FRANCO ✦ N FRANCOIS ✦ D FRANKLIN ✦ J FRANKLIN ✦ P FREEMAN ✦ G FRENCH ✦ M FRENCH ✦ D FRENCH ✦ R FRIDO ✦ N FROGLEY ✦ J FRONDA ✦ T FUFEYIN ✦ J FULLER ✦ P FULLER ✦ D FURDUIU ✦ Z FURKA ✦ D FURLONG ✦ M FUSTEI ✦ P GABRIEL ✦ R GADRUS ✦ A GAFFARENA ✦ L GAFITA ✦ P GAGER ✦ G GAHTA ✦ K GAILIUNAS ✦ M GAIZAUSKIENE ✦ J GALEA ✦ S GALIULIN ✦ M GALLAGHER ✦ P GALLAGHER ✦ F GALLAGHER ✦ J GALVIN ✦ A GANCHEV ✦ A GAPEJEVAS ✦ S GARAGHTY ✦ I GARAIS ✦ L GARCIA ✦ M GARCZYK ✦ A GARDINER ✦ S GARDNER ✦ C GAREPO ✦ J GARLAND ✦ C GARNETT ✦ J GARRATT ✦ N GARRATT ✦ B GARRETT ✦ X GASHI ✦ A GASIUNAS ✦ P GASIUNAS ✦ P GAUGHAN ✦ A GAUNT ✦ B GAVIN ✦ A GAWOR ✦ D GAYLE ✦ S GAYLE ✦ I GEAMANU ✦ A GEAR ✦ B GEBORSKI ✦ M GEDDES ✦ P GEE ✦ R GEE ✦ C GELDARD ✦ C GELDER ✦ R GELZINIS ✦ P GENT ✦ V GENUSE ✦ A GEORGE ✦ G GEORGHITA ✦ G GEORGIEV ✦ R GEORGIEV ✦ V GEORGIEV ✦ M GEORGIEV ✦ M GERMIN ✦ T GETOV ✦ K GHALE ✦ L GHEORGHE ✦ R GHEORGHE ✦ B GHEORGHITA ✦ P GHIATA ✦ V GHIORGHIAT ✦ S GHITA ✦ G GIANANTONIO ✦ D GIBBS ✦ S GIBBS ✦ M GIBSON ✦ I GIBSON ✦ D GIDDINGS ✦ I GIDLEY ✦ G GILBERTSON ✦ R GILKES ✦ S GILKES ✦ B GILL ✦ F GILL ✦ E GILLEAD ✦ P GILLESPIE ✦ D GILMORE ✦ C GINGA ✦ S GINGELL ✦ M GINNS ✦ D GIORGOU ✦ L GIRJAN ✦ V GIZUEKIS ✦ D GLACKIN ✦ C GLAZIER ✦ A GLAZOV ✦ S GLEESON ✦ D GLEESON ✦ N GLEESON ✦ D GLOVER ✦ J GLOVER ✦ M GLOWACKI ✦ D GODDARD ✦ S GODDARD ✦ L GOGGIN ✦ M GOLDA ✦ D GOLDYN ✦ Z GOLEBIOWSI ✦ K GOLEBIOWSKI ✦ E GOODE ✦ A GOODE ✦ B GOODE ✦ E GOODE ✦ D GOODERE ✦ K GOODFELLOW ✦ S GOODFELLOW ✦ D GOODMAN ✦ R GOODMEW ✦ J GOODSON ✦ A GORAL ✦ K GORDAN ✦ T GORDON ✦ A GORDON ✦ M GORDON ✦ T GORGIOSKI ✦ R GORICHA ✦ F GORKA ✦ P GOROVNIOVAS ✦ I GOUGH ✦ T GOW ✦ G GRAHAM ✦ C GRAHAM ✦ L GRAHAM ✦ P GRAINGER ✦ D GRANAHAN ✦ A GRANDEA ✦ D GRANT ✦ C GRASU ✦ R GRATTAN ✦ J GRAVLIK ✦ K GRAY ✦ P GRAY ✦ I GRECEA ✦ M GRECU ✦ V GRECU ✦ A GREEN ✦ C GREEN ✦ C GREEN ✦ D GREEN ✦ G GREEN ✦ J GREEN ✦ M GREEN ✦ D GREENE ✦ M GREENE ✦ A GREENHALGH ✦ J GREENHALGH ✦ O GREENLAND ✦ M GREENLAND ✦ G GREENSMITH ✦ B GREER ✦ R GREGOIRE ✦ S GREGORY ✦ D GREGORY ✦ D GREY ✦ B GRIFFITHS ✦ G GRIFFITHS ✦ K GRIFFITHS ✦ D GRIFFITHS ✦ A GRIGORE ✦ C GROENEWALD ✦ J GROMOL ✦ B GROSS ✦ L GROSS ✦ N GROSS ✦ M GROZDEV ✦ I GRSHAM ✦ K GRUCA ✦ P GRUMBLE ✦ V GUCEANU ✦ C GUERRERO ✦ A GUEST ✦ S GUNN ✦ T GUNN ✦ K GURAUSKAS ✦ A GURSCHI ✦ I GUTE ✦ A GUTON ✦ C GYAMFI ✦ S GYAN ✦ J HAASTRUP ✦ N HACKETT ✦ J HADDON ✦ J HAGANS ✦ S HAGGER ✦ M HAGGERTY ✦ R HAIDARI ✦ S HAINES ✦ J HAINSBOROUGH ✦ G HAKA ✦ J HALDES ✦ R HALFORD ✦ F HALL ✦ P HALL ✦ F HALL ✦ T HALL ✦ T HALLAM ✦ D HALLAS ✦ N HALLIDAY ✦ S HALLORAN ✦ J HALSEY ✦ B HAMILTON ✦ S HAMILTON ✦ D HAMLYN ✦ J HAMMOND ✦ M HAMMOND ✦ T HAMMOND ✦ H HAND ✦ T HANDS ✦ M HANLON ✦ A HANNA ✦

H HANRATTY ✦ E HANSFORD ✦ A HARAS ✦ J HARDING ✦ J HARDING ✦ T HARDING ✦ D HARDWICK ✦ D HARHAS ✦ C HARIAN ✦ M HARIN ✦ A HARNWELL ✦ D HARRADINE ✦ M HARRIS ✦ P HARRIS ✦ P HARRIS ✦ S HARRIS ✦ C HARRISON ✦ W HARRISON ✦ S HARRISON ✦ L HARRISON ✦ L HARRY ✦ G HART ✦ J HART ✦ C HART ✦ G HART ✦ B HARTIN ✦ M HARTLEY ✦ K HARTON-SZABOLCS ✦ S HARVEY ✦ N HARVEY ✦ P HARVEY ✦ G HASSAN ✦ H HASSAN ✦ S HATCHER ✦ S HATTINGH ✦ M HATTLEY ✦ H HAUGHTON ✦ D HAWES ✦ A HAWKE ✦ N HAWKES ✦ P HAWKINS ✦ A HAYDEN ✦ A HAYDEN ✦ P HAYDN ✦ G HAYES ✦ R HAYES ✦ R HAYES ✦ S HAYS ✦ A HAYTHORNTHWAITE ✦ M HAYWARD ✦ L HAYWARD ✦ E HAYWOOD ✦ D HEAD ✦ A HEAD ✦ J HEADLAND ✦ C HEALY ✦ M HEASMAN ✦ A HEAVER ✦ D HEAVER ✦ J HEAVER ✦ M HECKRATH ✦ A HECTOR ✦ M HEDGES ✦ T HEDGES ✦ J-M HEIDERSCHEID ✦ J HEISSL ✦ C HELPS ✦ D HENDERSON ✦ J HENDLE ✦ D HENMAN ✦ C HENRY ✦ S HENRY ✦ R HENRY ✦ J HEPPTING ✦ W HERBERT ✦ I HERBERT ✦ S HERON ✦ P HERSCHELL ✦ M HEXTALL ✦ M HEYWOOD ✦ D HICKEY ✦ P HICKEY ✦ S HICKIN ✦ M HICKS ✦ T HIGGINS ✦ C HIGGINS ✦ A HIGGS ✦ D HIGGS ✦ D HIGGS ✦ A HILL ✦ J HILL ✦ L HILL ✦ R HILL L ✦ S HILL ✦ C HILLARY ✦ A HILLIARD ✦ D HILLIER ✦ R HILLMAN ✦ P HILTON ✦ P HILTON ✦ S HINDLEY ✦ M HINZ ✦ R HIRANI ✦ P HIRTSCH ✦ T HOBBS ✦ W HOCKETT ✦ M HODGSON ✦ B HOEY ✦ P HOFER ✦ M HOGAN ✦ N HOGAN ✦ G HOGGER ✦ M HOKEY ✦ K HOLDEN ✦ M HOLDER ✦ J HOLE ✦ D HOLLAND ✦ J HOLLANDS ✦ B HOLLINGSWORTH ✦ B HOLLOBONE ✦ M HOLLOWAY ✦ B HOLMAN ✦ B HOLMES ✦ M HOLMES ✦ M HOLMES ✦ V HOLMOGOROVS ✦ S HOLNESS ✦ G HOMER ✦ C HOMOCEA ✦ P HOOD ✦ J HOOK ✦ J HOOPER ✦ J HOOPER ✦ M HOOPER ✦ A HORAN ✦ S HORAN ✦ V HORMIERE ✦ T HORSLEY ✦ B HORTON ✦ K HOSIER ✦ K HOUGHTON ✦ T HOUSE ✦ B HOWARD ✦ D HOWARD ✦ B HOWE ✦ C HOWE ✦ J HOWE ✦ K HOWES ✦ G HOWLEY ✦ K HOXHA ✦ I HRISTOV ✦ M HRISTOV ✦ H HTET ✦ L HUCKLE ✦ M HUDOWKZ ✦ R HUDSON ✦ A HUGHES ✦ D HUGHES ✦ J HUGHES ✦ J HUGHES ✦ J HUGHES ✦ P HUGHES ✦ T HUGHES ✦ L HUI ✦ S HULL ✦ P HUMBY ✦ M HUME ✦ J HUMMERSTON ✦ D HUMPHREY ✦ J HUNT ✦ D HUNTLEY ✦ M HUPA ✦ B HURLEY ✦ M HURST ✦ L HUSE ✦ D HUSE ✦ A HUSEEN ✦ M HUTCHINSON ✦ J HUTCHINSON ✦ M HUTCHINSON ✦ J HUTTLESTONE ✦ D HYDE ✦ A IBBESON ✦ V IBEAWLCHI ✦ A IBIKUNLE ✦ P ICHIM ✦ N IDAROLA ✦ S IDOWU ✦ E IFFIE ✦ A IHEANACHO ✦ B ILAS ✦ N ILESOI ✦ J ILETT ✦ M ILIE ✦ D ILISOI ✦ M ILISOI ✦ B ILORI ✦ S ILORI ✦ G ILSLEY ✦ V IMENICKAS ✦ M INCLES ✦ N INGLE ✦ B IOAM SEBASTIAN ✦ C IOAN ✦ B ION ADRIAN ✦ D IONCIU ✦ L IONEL ✦ I IONESCU ✦ T IONESCU ✦ M IONITA ✦ V IONITA ✦ C IONITOAEI ✦ B IONUT ✦ I IORDAN ✦ M IORI ✦ F IOSIF ✦ R IOSIF ✦ C IRELAND ✦ J IRELAND ✦ M IRELAND ✦ D IRVING ✦ K IRVING ✦ T IRWIN ✦ P ISAJEV ✦ A ISHERWOOD ✦ D ISHERWOOD ✦ R ISMAILOV ✦ J ISTED ✦ A IVANOV ✦ I IVANOV ✦ I IVANOV ✦ M IVANOV ✦ M IVANOV ✦ Y IVANOV ✦ A IZDONAS ✦ M JACISKO ✦ J JACKSON ✦ M JACKSON ✦ S JACKUS ✦ A JADESKA ✦ N JAGO ✦ A JAKOVLEVAS ✦ P JALES ✦ D JALLOH ✦ M JAMAL ✦ J JAMES ✦ H JANA ✦ P JANAS ✦ D JANCZUK ✦ M JANICKI ✦ P JANIK ✦ G JANKUNAS ✦ N JANOS ✦ R JANOSEVICIUS ✦ M JANOWSKI ✦ L JANUSZKIEWICZ ✦ L JAQUES ✦ P JARMAN ✦ J JAROSLAVIENE ✦ L JARVIS ✦ V JASAS ✦ Z JASICZEK ✦ A JAVED ✦ P JAYE ✦ S JEFCOATE ✦ G JEKAJ ✦ M JENKINS ✦ C JENNER ✦ A JENNINGS ✦ C JOBRE ✦ S JOCYS ✦ V JODKA ✦ S JOE ✦ P JOHN ✦ S JOHN ✦ B JOHNSON ✦ C JOHNSON ✦ G JOHNSON ✦ J JOHNSON ✦ M JOHNSON ✦ M JOHNSON ✦ R JOHNSON ✦ S JOHNSON ✦ S JOHNSON ✦ A JOHNSTON ✦ B JOHNSTON ✦ S JOHNSTON ✦ G JOKUBAUSKAS ✦ A JONES ✦ C JONES ✦ D JONES ✦ J JONES ✦ L JONES ✦ M JONES ✦ P JONES ✦ T JONES ✦ M JOSEPH ✦ B JOSIAH ✦ N JOYCE ✦ E JOYCE ✦ D JUCIANSZ ✦ A JUDD ✦ D JUDGE ✦ P JUDGE ✦ D JUGE ✦ M JUHASZ ✦ V JURKONIS ✦ S JUSTICE ✦ P KAAYA ✦ A KACHUZ ✦ T KACZMAREK ✦ G KACZOR ✦ J KAISER ✦ H KAISSI ✦ K KALAPAN ✦ R KALINOWSKI ✦ V KALLAI ✦ A KALPOKAS ✦ T KALUDOV ✦ U KANU ✦ K KAPLA ✦ B KARASINSKI ✦ A KARBOWIAK ✦ V KARCIAUSKAS ✦ G KARCIAUSKAS ✦ A KARDINSKI ✦ A KARIM ✦ E KARPIS ✦ K KARSKI ✦ M KARSKI ✦ Y KASABOU ✦ L KASILIAUSKAITE ✦ V KASPARAVICIUS ✦ A KASPARAVICIUS ✦ K KASPERSKI ✦ R KAVALAUSKAS ✦ O KAVANAGH ✦ S KAWA ✦ W KEATING ✦ R KEATING ✦ P KEE ✦ J KEEGAN ✦ D KEETCH ✦ J KEHINDE ✦ G KEIR ✦ S KELLEHER ✦ M KELLEHER ✦ J KELLER ✦ A KELLMAN ✦ A KELLY ✦ B KELLY ✦ J KELLY ✦ J KELLY ✦ L KELLY ✦ R KELLY ✦ R KELLY ✦ S KELLY ✦ E KEMEL ✦ T KEMPTON ✦ R KENDALL ✦ P KENNA ✦ M KENNEDY ✦ J KENNEDY ✦ C KENNELLY ✦ T KENNELLY ✦ L KENNY ✦ M KENNY ✦ R KENNY ✦ J KENT ✦ J KENT-SMITH ✦ R KENWAY ✦ V KERAI ✦ T KERELODI ✦ M KERR ✦ I KERWICK ✦ V KFTERIUS ✦ A KHABIBULLAEV ✦ A KHALIL ✦ S KHAN ✦ S KHAN ✦ A KHETANI ✦ G KIDD ✦ M KIELY ✦ A KILANI ✦ D KILBEY ✦ F KILBEY ✦ D KILLINGBACK ✦ E KINDEREVICIUS ✦ C KING ✦ E KING ✦ F KING ✦ L KING ✦ P KING ✦ S KING ✦ B KIRBY ✦ R KIRBY ✦ K KIRILOV ✦ V KIRILOV ✦ S KIRSOP ✦ A KIRVELAITIS ✦ M KITT ✦ N KKAFAS ✦ J KLEIOVS ✦ W KLIMA ✦ K KLIMA ✦ D KNAPP ✦ M KNIGHT ✦ M KNIGHT ✦ B KNOWLES ✦ R KNOWLES ✦ E KOCHEV ✦ T KOCIMSKI ✦ J KONDRATEWKO ✦ A KOONER ✦ R KOPROWSKI ✦ M KORBET ✦ K KOREPTA ✦ V KOROBTSOV ✦ V KOSOLAPOV ✦ A KOSTEWICZ ✦ T KOSZALKA ✦ T KOWALCZYK ✦ S KOYCHEV ✦ S KOZERA ✦ A KOZKA ✦ A KOZLOWSKI ✦ K KOZUBSKI ✦ M KRAKOWSKI ✦ D KRASTEV ✦ K KRASTEV ✦ N KROMAH ✦ M KRZEMINSKI ✦ S KUDAH ✦ P KULWICKI ✦ M KUPIEC ✦ M KUPKA ✦ D KURTI ✦ I KURTI ✦ T KURTI ✦ L KUSZPIT ✦ A KWIATEK ✦ I KYOSEV ✦ L LABUDA ✦ I LABZENTIS ✦ C LACATIS ✦ R LAFFAN ✦ J LAGNOVSKIS ✦ A LAKEMAN ✦ R LAKEN ✦ A LAKIN ✦ T LAKOMIEC ✦ J LAMB ✦ N LAMB ✦ O LAMB ✦ M LAMBANCUIC ✦ G LAMBERT ✦ L LAMBETH ✦ D LAMMIMAN ✦ E LANE ✦ J LANE ✦ D LANGFORD ✦ J LANGFORD ✦ A LANGSTEAD ✦ G LANGSTON ✦ S LANSBERG ✦ E LAOGUN ✦ G LAPKOV ✦ M LAPPER ✦ A LAPUNOVS ✦ E LARBI-MENSAH ✦ S LATHEN ✦ D LAUEZZARI ✦ J LAUREL ✦ T LAVERACK ✦ A LAWAL ✦ F LAWAL ✦ D LAWERENCE ✦ P LAWERENCE ✦ M LAWLESS ✦ R LAWLESS ✦ W LAWNIK ✦ L LAWRENCE ✦ N LAWRIE ✦ B LAWSON ✦ I LAWSON ✦ R LAWSON ✦ C LAY ✦ J LAY ✦ P LAY ✦ J LAYBOURN ✦ C LAZAR ✦ I LAZAR ✦ P LAZAR ✦ R LAZAR ✦ B LAZAROV ✦ R LAZARUS ✦ M LEA ✦ G LEADBEATER ✦ S LEAHY ✦ M LEARY ✦ A LEE ✦ J LEE ✦ J LEE ✦ J LEE ✦ J LEE ✦ K LEE ✦ M LEE ✦ M LEE ✦ R LEE ✦ A LEGGETT ✦ T LEHMANN ✦ A LEKA ✦ B LEMANI ✦ M LEMANOWICZ ✦ B LENGYEL ✦ J LENNOX ✦ L LEOPOLD ✦ J LESHOMMES ✦ A LESLIE ✦ M LESPERANCE ✦ R LESUN ✦ M LETCH ✦ C LEVETT ✦ S LEVETT ✦ M LEWANDOWSKI ✦ M LEWIN ✦ A LEWIS ✦ C LEWIS ✦ G LEWIS ✦ J LEWIS ✦ N LEWIS ✦ R LEWIS ✦ A LICHACZ ✦ V LIGEIKA ✦ N LIGHT ✦ V LIKANIS ✦ S LILLY ✦ C LIMGORAR ✦ C LINES ✦ J LING ✦ J LING ✦ S LING ✦ T LING ✦ L LINGE ✦ R LINTON ✦ M LISI ✦ M LISIECKA ✦ T LISOWSKI ✦ G LITTLE ✦ G LITTLE ✦ V LIUTKUS ✦ D LIVIU ✦ J LOBRY ✦ S LOCKER ✦ C LOCKYER ✦ D LOCKYER ✦ M LODDER ✦ H LOEKKEN ✦ M LOFTUS ✦ M LOGAN ✦ A LOGES ✦ P LOMUTI ✦ D LONDON ✦ Z LONDON ✦ S LONGHURST ✦ D LORINTI ✦ G LOTFIAN ✦ P LOUDON ✦ S LOVE ✦ D LOVETT ✦ W LOVETT ✦ A LOWE ✦ D LOWE ✦ T LOWE ✦ T LOWE ✦ K LOWERS ✦ A LOWTEH ✦ M LUCA ✦ B LUCAS ✦ D LUCAS ✦ D LUCAS ✦ S LUCIAN ✦ K LUDLAM ✦ B LUGG ✦ S LUKEY ✦ I LUKOSEVICIUS ✦ D LUKOSIUS ✦ V LUKSANS ✦ A LUNCA ✦ K LUTHERS ✦ A LYNOTT ✦ D LYONS

✦ A LYSTER ✦ P MABY ✦ C MACCORMACK ✦ A MACDONALD ✦ D MACDONALD ✦ F MACDONALD ✦ K MACDONALD ✦ K MACDONALD ✦ S MACDONALD ✦ T MACK ✦ K MACKEW ✦ D MACLEAN ✦ A MACLENNAN ✦ R MACOVEI ✦ A MADDOCK ✦ R MADDRELL ✦ V MADJOUNOV ✦ D MADZHUNOV ✦ C MAGDICI ✦ D MAISEY ✦ G MAISEY ✦ K MAISEY ✦ I MAJOR ✦ R MAJUS ✦ E MAKARAS ✦ B MALAMTOJE ✦ W MALARZ ✦ A MALCOM ✦ C MALE ✦ H MALEK ✦ B MALONE ✦ C MALONEY ✦ B MALPASS ✦ C MALYSZKO ✦ J MAMBAKASA ✦ A MANAHAN ✦ P MANKELLOW ✦ M MANN ✦ R MANN ✦ M MANNERS ✦ L MANNING ✦ K MANSFIELD ✦ B MANSFIELD ✦ J MANTO ✦ S MANTU ✦ T MANU ✦ A MANZOOR ✦ C MARAIS ✦ L MARCELLE ✦ R MARCINKEVICIUS ✦ D MARCU ✦ R MARCU ✦ D MARDARE ✦ M MARECKI ✦ B MAREK ✦ D MARES ✦ J MARFO ✦ V MARGEAN ✦ T MARIAN ✦ J MARINER ✦ H MARIUS-IMI ✦ M MARKOV ✦ P MARKS ✦ R MARKWELL ✦ R MARKWELL ✦ A MAROF ✦ L MARONGIU-MILLERSHIP ✦ D MARQUES ✦ C MARSH ✦ G MARSH ✦ J MARSH ✦ P MARSH ✦ S MARSH ✦ P MARSHALL ✦ R MARSHALL ✦ D MARSON ✦ M MARTIC ✦ A MARTIN ✦ G MARTIN ✦ L MARTIN ✦ L MARTIN ✦ M MARTIN ✦ M MARTIN ✦ N MARTIN ✦ R MARTIN ✦ K MARTISIUS ✦ D MARUSINEC ✦ R MARVEN ✦ V MASARA ✦ S MASCHIO ✦ L MASEK ✦ J MASON ✦ M MASON ✦ M MASSIAH ✦ D MASUR ✦ B MASYSZKA ✦ A MATEESCU ✦ A MATERYNSKYY ✦ D MATOCHA ✦ J MATOS ✦ P MATSKIV ✦ A MATTHEW ✦ R MATTHEWS ✦ S MATTIL ✦ M MATUK ✦ P MATUK ✦ P MAUGHAN ✦ P MAURIZIO ✦ C MAX ✦ D MAXWELL ✦ T MAXWELL ✦ G MAY ✦ S MAY ✦ P MAYBANK ✦ R MAYBANK ✦ B MAYER ✦ T MAYNARD ✦ M MAZILU ✦ O MAZITOV ✦ W MCADAM ✦ A MCARTHUR ✦ T MCCABE ✦ T MCCALLAN ✦ B MCCARTHY ✦ J MCCARTHY ✦ K MCCARTHY ✦ L MCCARTHY ✦ S MCCARTHY ✦ F MCCAUL ✦ M MCCAUL ✦ J MCCAULEY ✦ D MCCLEOD ✦ D MCCOLGAN ✦ G MCCOMB ✦ M MCCORMACK ✦ S MCCORMICK ✦ M MCCRAE ✦ K MCCULLAGH ✦ G MCCULLUGH ✦ S MCDAID ✦ S MCDERMOTT ✦ C MCDONALD ✦ B MCDONNELL ✦ T MCDONNELL ✦ N MCDOUGALL ✦ J MCELLIGOTT ✦ R MCFARLANE ✦ J MCGACHAN ✦ S MCGEEVER ✦ G MCGIFFEN ✦ J MCGILL ✦ J MCGLEN ✦ R MCGLOUGHLIN ✦ P MCGOWAN ✦ V MCGRATH ✦ C MCGREGOR ✦ C MCGREGOR ✦ J MCGROARTY ✦ B MCGUIGAN ✦ G MCGUINESS ✦ J MCGUINESS ✦ A MCGUIRE ✦ M MCHUGH ✦ A MCKAY ✦ O MCKENLEY ✦ P MCKENNA ✦ R MCKENNA ✦ D MCKENZIE ✦ S MCKERNAN ✦ I MCKINNON ✦ B MCLAUGHLIN ✦ K MCLAUGHLIN ✦ L MCLEISH ✦ R MCLEN ✦ K MCLEOD ✦ N MCLOUGHLIN ✦ S MCLOUGHLIN ✦ D MCMAHON ✦ C MCMILLAN ✦ L MCNABB ✦ P MCNALLY ✦ A MCNAMARA ✦ J MCNAMARA ✦ M MCNAMARA ✦ M MCNAMARA ✦ S MCPADDEN ✦ W MCPAKE ✦ S MCQUEEN ✦ A MCWATERS ✦ A MEAD ✦ J MEADE ✦ I MEDANESE ✦ F MEDEIROS ✦ W MEDZIAK ✦ I MEGYESI ✦ S MEHMEDOV ✦ J MELLOR ✦ I MENSAH ✦ C MERRIN ✦ J MERRITT ✦ D MESAROS ✦ K METCALFE ✦ D MEW ✦ F MEXTED ✦ D MICHALSKI ✦ M MICHI ✦ S MIDDLEMASS ✦ F MIFTARI ✦ D MIGAS ✦ Z MIGONIS ✦ C MIHAI ✦ C MIHAI ✦ C MIHAILESCU ✦ C MIHALACHE ✦ S MIHAYLOV ✦ R MIKALAUSKAS ✦ D MIKOLAJCZAK ✦ A MIKULENAS ✦ I MILBOURN ✦ D MILBURN ✦ R MILES ✦ C MILLAR ✦ S MILLAR ✦ A MILLARD ✦ P MILLARD ✦ S MILLEN ✦ D MILLER ✦ J MILLER ✦ J MILLER ✦ K MILLER ✦ N MILLER ✦ P MILLER ✦ A MILLS ✦ C MILLS ✦ D MILLS ✦ J MILLS ✦ M MILLS ✦ M MILLS ✦ D MILLWARD ✦ A MILUTIS ✦ R MIMONI ✦ D MINCHEV ✦ J MINDAUAGAS ✦ J MINGARD ✦ J MINGLE ✦ R MINGLE ✦ L MINKEVICIUS ✦ F MINTO ✦ Z MIRON ✦ K MIROSLAW ✦ M MISCHE ✦ L MISIEWICZ ✦ N MISINI ✦ A MISKOW ✦ A MITCHELL ✦ C MITCHELL ✦ J MITCHELL ✦ J MITCHELL ✦ R MITCHELL ✦ S MITCHELL ✦ V MITUSHEVA ✦ C MOCA ✦ S MOCKA ✦ A MODRZEJEWSKI ✦ S MOGA ✦ M MOLDOVAN ✦ W MOLE ✦ S MOLLOV ✦ K MOLONEY ✦ J MONCRIEFF ✦ R MONERO ✦ T MONERO ✦ R MONETA ✦ K MONGER ✦ M MONK ✦ M MONKS ✦ A MONTAGUE ✦ B MONTAGUE ✦ J MONTEIRO ✦ D MONTIER ✦ P MOONEY ✦ C MOORE ✦ K MOORE ✦ L MOORE ✦ N MOORE ✦ R MOORE ✦ D MORALIEV ✦ A MORAN ✦ G MORCOMBE ✦ T MORDUANT ✦ V MOREIRA ✦ B MORFETT ✦ C MORGAN ✦ D MORGAN ✦ G MORGAN ✦ J MORGAN ✦ K MORGAN ✦ L MORGAN ✦ W MORGAN ✦ B MORIATY ✦ G MORING ✦ O MOROZA ✦ A MORRIS ✦ B MORRIS ✦ C MORRIS ✦ J MORRIS ✦ D MORRISON ✦ E MORRISSON ✦ M MORT ✦ A MORTON ✦ T MORTON ✦ C MOSELEY ✦ T MOSES ✦ I MOSNEAGU ✦ R MOSS ✦ O MOTHERSILL ✦ S MOULDER ✦ B MOUNTFORD ✦ A MOWBRAY ✦ J MOWBRAY ✦ H MOXOM ✦ S MOYNIHAN ✦ K MUCHA ✦ L MUDIE ✦ C MUHOLLAND ✦ J MUILANE ✦ J MUIR ✦ S MUIR ✦ B MULCAHY ✦ D MULCAHY ✦ K MULHOLLAND ✦ J MULLINGS ✦ D MULLINS ✦ S MUNDAY ✦ M MUNGROO ✦ I MUNRO ✦ C MUNTEANU ✦ C MUNTEANU ✦ I MUNTEANU ✦ I MUNTEANU ✦ N MUNTEANU ✦ J MURPHY ✦ K MURPHY ✦ L MURPHY ✦ P MURPHY ✦ P MURPHY ✦ R MURPHY ✦ E MURRAY ✦ K MURRAY ✦ C MURRELL ✦ G MURRELL ✦ S MUTTI ✦ S MYERS ✦ M MYNAN ✦ I MYNAR ✦ T NAATEY ✦ P NADEJDA ✦ M NAE ✦ D NARAN ✦ V NARARENKO ✦ V NARBUNTAS ✦ D NARDONE ✦ J NASH ✦ P NASH ✦ S NASH ✦ S NASH ✦ T NASH ✦ P NASM ✦ D NAUGHTON ✦ E NAVICKAS ✦ C NAYLOR ✦ A NDIAYE ✦ L NDUME ✦ J NEALE ✦ M NEASCU ✦ I NECULAI ✦ N NEDELCHEV ✦ K NEDYALKOV ✦ P NEE ✦ C NEGOITA ✦ B NELL ✦ C NELSON ✦ D NELSON ✦ V NELSON ✦ Z NEOLEV ✦ I NETHAWAY ✦ B NEWMAN ✦ T NEWMAN ✦ A NEWTON ✦ E NEZA ✦ E NG ✦ N NGUYEN ✦ R NIAURONIS ✦ G NIȘHIȚOI ✦ N NICHIȚOI ✦ J NICHOLLS ✦ C NICHOLS ✦ T NICHOLS ✦ G NICHOLSON ✦ S NICHOLSON ✦ S NICOL ✦ A NICOLAE ✦ G NICOLICIOIU ✦ M NIEDZIELA ✦ S NIKOLOU ✦ G NIKOLOV ✦ A NIMAKO ✦ A NISTOR ✦ M NISTOR ✦ F NITA ✦ J NKADI ✦ O NNADI ✦ G NOAKES ✦ L NOBLE ✦ R NOBREGA ✦ H NOEL ✦ J NOKES ✦ K NOLAN ✦ J NORKETT ✦ J NORKETT ✦ B NORMAN ✦ J NORMAN ✦ L NORRIS ✦ A NORTH ✦ D NORTH ✦ P NORTHCLIFFE ✦ W NORTON ✦ D NORWOOD ✦ J NOVAK ✦ D NOWAK ✦ P NOWAK ✦ R NOWICKI ✦ B NOYCE ✦ D NOYCE ✦ R NOZDRIN ✦ P NOZKA ✦ D NUNN ✦ P NURDEN ✦ S NURSE ✦ V NUTU ✦ D NWAFOR ✦ C NWAJEI ✦ U NWOKA ✦ C NWOSU ✦ E NWOYE ✦ V NWOYEOCHA ✦ A NYCYK ✦ A NYCYK ✦ D NZEKWE ✦ A OAKLEY ✦ C OAKLEY ✦ P OBIEKWE ✦ M OBOT ✦ A O'BRIEN ✦ J O'BRIEN ✦ R O'BRIEN ✦ B OBUTUYO ✦ T OCKENDON ✦ B O'CONNOR ✦ M O'CONNOR ✦ N ODDY ✦ V ODEKUNLE ✦ K ODHAV ✦ G O'DONNELL ✦ L O'DONNELL ✦ L O'DONNELL ✦ M O'DONOGHUE ✦ R O'DOWD ✦ A O'DRISCOLL ✦ O ODUALA ✦ A ODUJINRIN ✦ D ODUNTAN ✦ T O'FARRELL ✦ D OFITERU ✦ C OGBECHI ✦ A OGDEN ✦ S O'GORMAN ✦ G O'GUNDELE ✦ T OGUNJOBI ✦ J OGUNKEYEDE ✦ O OGUNKEYEDE ✦ F OGUNNUSI ✦ A OGUNTSIRU ✦ D OGUNYA ✦ M O'HARA ✦ S OHENLEN ✦ O OJEKUNLE ✦ A OJO ✦ A OJO ✦ J OKENYI ✦ C OKEZIE ✦ D OKOLI ✦ C OKORIE ✦ J OKORONKWO ✦ O OLA ✦ I OLADIPUPO ✦ A OLAITAN ✦ P OLECH ✦ G OLENIUC ✦ N OLENIUC ✦ P OLIVEIRA ✦ C OLIVER ✦ M OLIVER ✦ H O'LOUGHLIN ✦ K OMARA ✦ A OMER ✦ B ONCIU ✦ D ONCIU ✦ P O'NEIL-DWYER ✦ J O'NEILL ✦ R O'NEILL ✦ T ONOFREI ✦ S ONUH ✦ M ONUORA ✦ C ONWUGHARA ✦ M OPPONG ✦ P ORBAN ✦ K O'REILLY ✦ F OREL ✦ F ORIEKE ✦ V ORLOV ✦ A ORLOVS ✦ O ORMOND ✦ M ORTON ✦ A OSAE-AKONNOR ✦ C OSBORN ✦ C OSBOURNE ✦ E OSEI ✦ M OSEI-AMPONSAH ✦ J OSEI-AGYEMANG ✦ P O'SHEA ✦ T O'SHEA ✦ J OSINNOWO ✦ A OSINSKI ✦ M OSUJI ✦ B O'SULLIVAN ✦ N O'SULLIVAN ✦ B OVIDIU ✦ M OWCZAREK ✦ K OWCZAREK ✦ I OWEN ✦ J OWEN ✦ R OWEN ✦ D OWENS ✦ R OWUSU

✦ S OXLEY ✦ A PADELE ✦ B PAFFETT ✦ P PAGE ✦ C PAING ✦ D PAIZAN ✦ S PAKSKIS ✦ M PALADE ✦ D PALKA ✦ K PALLISTER ✦ A PALMER ✦ M PALMER ✦ S PALMER ✦ V PALMER ✦ L PANA ✦ M PANAINTE ✦ I PANDA ✦ H PANEDAR ✦ D PANIPUCCI ✦ J PANKHANIA ✦ M PANKHANIA ✦ D PANNELL ✦ G PAPADOPOULOS ✦ Y PAPADOPOULOS ✦ A PAPCIAK ✦ I PAPUC ✦ D PARAOARU ✦ V PARASCHIV ✦ J PARE ✦ B PARFENYUK ✦ A PARILLON ✦ B PARISH ✦ A PARKER ✦ A PARKER ✦ B PARKER ✦ B PARKER ✦ D PARKER ✦ P PARKER ✦ D PARKES ✦ J PARKES ✦ B PARKINSON ✦ S PARKINSON ✦ C PARPERI ✦ N PARRY ✦ P PARRY ✦ G PARTON ✦ R PASCA ✦ K PASCAL ✦ C PASCARU ✦ I PASEK ✦ R PASEK ✦ P PASKALEV ✦ R PASZKOWSKI ✦ A PASZKOWSKI ✦ H PATEL ✦ P PATEL ✦ R PATEL ✦ K PATERSON ✦ S PATO ✦ J PATON ✦ M PATRICK ✦ D PATTERSON ✦ M PATTERSON ✦ R PATTERSON ✦ J PATTINSON ✦ A PATWA ✦ I PAUKAUSKAS ✦ S PAUL ✦ T PAULIUE ✦ J PAVEY ✦ A PAVLOU ✦ I PAVLOV ✦ K PAWEL ✦ A PAYE ✦ B PAYNE ✦ D PAYNE ✦ J PEACHEY ✦ D PEAKE ✦ J PEAKE ✦ A PEARCE ✦ G PEARCE ✦ K PEARCE ✦ D PEARCEY ✦ T PEARSON ✦ S PEASE ✦ L PECIULIS ✦ K PECKYS ✦ A PEDRO ✦ A PEEK ✦ C PEGG ✦ E PEINADO ✦ D PELCZARSKI ✦ G PELGER ✦ D PEMBROKE ✦ J PENFOLD ✦ W PENKETH ✦ S PENN ✦ S PENNELL ✦ G PENSON ✦ J PENSON ✦ S PEPOSHI ✦ B PERAJ ✦ J PERCA ✦ B PERKINS ✦ D PERRY ✦ M PERSAUD ✦ J PETERO ✦ C PETERS ✦ S PETERSEN ✦ V PETKEVICIUS ✦ A PETRAUSKAS ✦ M PETRE ✦ P PETRICA ✦ D PETROV ✦ I PETROV ✦ I PETROV ✦ M PETTIT ✦ D PETZNER ✦ G PHILLIPS ✦ J PHILLIPS ✦ M PHILLIPS ✦ O PHILLIPS ✦ S PHILLIPS ✦ T PHILLIPS ✦ M PHILLISKIRK ✦ M PIECHA ✦ R PIEKYS ✦ J PIELASZKIEWICZ ✦ D PIERCE ✦ J PIETRAS ✦ K PINAULT ✦ R PINCHES ✦ M PINTHE ✦ F PIPER ✦ S PIPER ✦ G PIRES ✦ E PIRRI ✦ F PIRVU ✦ A PISLARIU ✦ J PITCHER ✦ D PIZEWSKI ✦ C PLAMADA ✦ J PLATT ✦ S PLAYER ✦ R PLUMB ✦ L PLUMRIDGE ✦ W PLUTA ✦ S PLYWACZ ✦ M PODKOWKA ✦ K POGORZELSKI ✦ V POICE ✦ T POKORSKI ✦ M POKRYWKA ✦ A POLLOCK ✦ G POLLOCK ✦ S POMROY ✦ J POND ✦ J POOLE ✦ T POOLE ✦ C POPA ✦ E POPA ✦ T POPA ✦ K POPE ✦ R POPE ✦ O POPESCU ✦ I POPOVICI ✦ R POPOVICI ✦ J PORTER ✦ T PORTER ✦ D PORWOL ✦ N POSENER ✦ S POSKITT ✦ P POTEPA ✦ B POTTER ✦ S POVEY ✦ A POWELL ✦ C POWELL ✦ P POWELL ✦ L POWERS ✦ N POYNTER ✦ R PRAJAPATI ✦ J PRASZCZALEK ✦ C PRAZER ✦ W PREMPEH ✦ J PRENDEGAST ✦ C PRENTICE ✦ A PRESTON ✦ B PRICE ✦ M PRICE ✦ M PRICE ✦ S PRICE ✦ V PRICE ✦ M PRIEKSAITIS ✦ A PRISACARU ✦ P PRITCHARD ✦ V PRODAN ✦ P PROGRI ✦ R PROMNY ✦ C PROMOROACA ✦ E PROUD ✦ L PROUD ✦ B PROUDFOOT ✦ P PRZEMYSLAW ✦ P PRZEPIORVA ✦ P PRZYWARA ✦ V PUHA ✦ R PURTON ✦ P PUSEY ✦ K QIRADAR ✦ R QUADJOVIE ✦ T QUARRY ✦ D QUAYE ✦ J QUICK ✦ J QUICK ✦ R QUINN ✦ I QURESHI ✦ R RABKOWSKI ✦ K RABKOWSKI ✦ A RACKETT ✦ F RAD ✦ D RADCLIFFE ✦ C RADESCU ✦ C RADLEY ✦ E RADOEV ✦ D RADOLA ✦ N RAGGHIANTI ✦ A RAHAMAN ✦ O RAINYS ✦ J RAMONA ✦ G RANICIA ✦ L RAPHAEL ✦ R RAPLEY ✦ U RARES ✦ A RASHID ✦ D RASIMAS ✦ J RAUSER ✦ T RAVEN ✦ C RAWORTH ✦ D RAYMOND ✦ J READ ✦ A REAPE ✦ T REDDIN ✦ N REDDIN ✦ S REDDY ✦ R REDFEARN ✦ C REDFERN ✦ M REDMOND ✦ J REDREARN ✦ P REECE ✦ D REED ✦ M REED ✦ M REED ✦ R REEVE ✦ M REEVES ✦ L REGINALDO ✦ C REID ✦ D REID ✦ M REID ✦ S REID ✦ D REILLY ✦ G REILLY ✦ N REILLY ✦ R REKASIUS ✦ M REYNOLDS ✦ M RHODEN ✦ C RHODES ✦ T RHODES ✦ R RIBEIRO ✦ A RICA ✦ E RICHARDS ✦ H RICHARDS ✦ J RICHARDS ✦ K RICHARDS ✦ L RICHARDS ✦ P RICHARDS ✦ A RICHARDSON ✦ J RICHARDSON ✦ R RICHARDSON ✦ G RICHENS ✦ M RICKARD ✦ S RIDER ✦ J RIDGWAY ✦ M RIGBY ✦ A RIMELIS ✦ R RIORDAN ✦ G RITCHIE ✦ J RITCHIE ✦ R RITCHIE ✦ S RITCHIE ✦ I RIZEA ✦ C ROBE ✦ I ROBERT ✦ E ROBERTS ✦ G ROBERTS ✦ K ROBERTS ✦ L ROBERTS ✦ L ROBERTS ✦ A ROBERTSON ✦ T ROBERTSON ✦ S ROBINSON ✦ S SCHLINDWEIN-ROBINSON ✦ R ROBINSON ✦ W ROBINSON ✦ B ROCHE ✦ J ROCHE ✦ A ROCHON ✦ P-Y ROCHON ✦ A RODRIGUEZ ✦ E RODRIEGUEZ ✦ C ROE ✦ L ROGERS ✦ G ROGOWSKI ✦ A ROMAN ✦ A ROMAN ✦ R ROMAN ✦ M ROOTSEY ✦ P ROSCOW ✦ R ROSS ✦ R ROSSALL ✦ P ROSSETTI ✦ D ROSSLEE ✦ L ROUST ✦ C ROWE ✦ D ROWE ✦ H ROWE ✦ K ROWE ✦ R ROWE ✦ S ROWE ✦ J ROWLEY ✦ P ROXBOROUGH ✦ R ROZENBERGS ✦ R RUMMELL ✦ V RUS ✦ R RUSECKAS ✦ H RUSEV ✦ S RUSHEN ✦ A RUSSELL ✦ J RUSSELL ✦ J RUSSELL ✦ R RUSSELL ✦ R RUSSELL ✦ S RUSSETT ✦ C RUSU ✦ M RUSU ✦ R RUTECUI ✦ D RUTTER ✦ J RYAN ✦ S RYAN ✦ S RYAN ✦ N RYDEK ✦ S SABBIR ✦ R SABHARWAL ✦ S SABULIS ✦ T SACCHETTO ✦ M SACH ✦ S SADIQ ✦ S SAIDOLIMOV ✦ R SAIGEMAN ✦ L SAKALAUSKAS ✦ D SAKOWSKI ✦ C SALSBURY ✦ I SAMES ✦ O SAMSON ✦ S SAMUEL ✦ A SAMUSEVS ✦ J SANDERSON ✦ E SANDLES ✦ J SANDREJ ✦ D SANDS ✦ D SANKEY ✦ N SANTER ✦ J SANTOS ✦ M SANTOS ✦ O SAROSLAVAS ✦ M SAUNDERS ✦ M SAUNDERS ✦ M SAUNDERS ✦ R SAUNDERS ✦ L SAVAGE ✦ M SAVILL ✦ A SCARLETT ✦ A SCHAUB ✦ A SCHAUB ✦ J SCHLETTE ✦ C SCHLOSS ✦ M SCHOLFIELD ✦ J SCHULTYE ✦ M SCILLE ✦ R SCISLOWSKI ✦ R SCOLA ✦ A SCOTT ✦ A SCOTT ✦ J SCOTT ✦ P SCOTT ✦ P SCOTT ✦ R SCOTT ✦ S SCOTT ✦ S SCRIBBINS ✦ L SCULLY ✦ T SEARLE ✦ H SEBASTIAN ✦ P SEEMAN ✦ A SEFERI ✦ T SEFERI ✦ M SEFULESEU ✦ C SEKYIREH ✦ R SELF ✦ L SELLERS ✦ D SEMENJUK ✦ R SEMMENS ✦ D SEMPER-HUGHES ✦ V SENKUS ✦ L SEQUEIRA ✦ A SERBAN ✦ D SEREICIKAS ✦ F SERGEONT ✦ S SERGICS ✦ S SERGIDES ✦ S SEVCISIN ✦ P SEWELL ✦ G SEYMOUR ✦ C SHARKEY ✦ S SHARP ✦ T SHAUZE ✦ E SHAW ✦ M SHAW ✦ T SHAW ✦ A SHAYLE ✦ R SHEAF ✦ S SHEAF ✦ P SHEARER ✦ N SHELDON ✦ S SHELLEY ✦ S SHELLEY ✦ S SHELLEY ✦ C SHEPHERD ✦ G SHEPPARD ✦ C SHEREMETOV ✦ G SHERLOCK ✦ A SHILLING ✦ P SHIPWAY ✦ M SHOBAMOND ✦ D SHOESMITH ✦ S SHOKRZADEH ✦ D SHOREY ✦ D SHORTALL ✦ A SHORTER ✦ L SHRIGLEY ✦ M SHRODER ✦ L SHUFFLEBOTHAM ✦ C SHUTE ✦ R SHUTTLEWOOD ✦ K SIBILSKI ✦ R SICKLEMORE ✦ S SIEMKO ✦ P SILVESTER ✦ G SILVIU ✦ I SIME ✦ A SIMMONDS ✦ M SIMMONDS ✦ M SIMMS ✦ M SIMONOWICZ ✦ K SIMONS ✦ M SIMPSON ✦ M SIMPSON ✦ A SIM ✦ L SIMSS ✦ G SINGH ✦ J SINGH ✦ R SINGH ✦ T SINGH ✦ B SINGLETON ✦ S SISIE ✦ M SISSONS ✦ M SITAHALL ✦ R SITCH ✦ V SKARNA ✦ H SKELTON ✦ K SKIBNIEWSKI ✦ E SKINMORE ✦ O SKINNER ✦ R SKINNER ✦ R SKINSLEY ✦ M SKITTRALL ✦ A SKOWRONSKI ✦ T SKUKAUSKAS ✦ M SKULL ✦ J SKYELS ✦ W SLACK ✦ R SLAVINSKAS ✦ D SLAVKOV ✦ P SLOAN ✦ M SLOBODZIAN ✦ E SLORA ✦ A SLYTER ✦ B SMALLCOMBE ✦ H SMALLCOMBE ✦ S SMALLCOMBE ✦ J SMALLWOOD ✦ M SMEESTERS ✦ M SMETZER ✦ R SMIERZYNSKI ✦ G SMIT ✦ B SMITH ✦ C SMITH ✦ C SMITH ✦ C SMITH ✦ C SMITH ✦ C SMITH ✦ D SMITH ✦ D SMITH ✦ D SMITH ✦ D SMITH ✦ D SMITH ✦ D SMITH ✦ E SMITH ✦ G SMITH ✦ J SMITH ✦ J SMITH ✦ J SMITH ✦ J SMITH ✦ I SMITH ✦ L SMITH ✦ L SMITH ✦ M SMITH ✦ M SMITH ✦ N SMITH ✦ N SMITH ✦ P SMITH ✦ P SMITH ✦ P SMITH ✦ R SMITH ✦ R SMITH ✦ S SMITH ✦ W SMITH ✦ D SNEE ✦ J SNELL ✦ J SNELL ✦ R SNIUKSTA ✦ A SNOW ✦ L SOBANSKI ✦ P SODEN ✦ A SOFFE ✦ S SOLLIS ✦ L SOLOMON ✦ P SOLOMON ✦ S SOLOMAN ✦ V SOPON ✦ M SOREA ✦ P SOSNOWSKI ✦ A SOUAN ✦ J SOYKA ✦ D SPAHU ✦ M SPAHU ✦ M SPAKAUSKAS ✦ D SPARKS ✦ L SPASSOVA ✦ I SPATARU ✦ B SPEARING ✦ J SPENCE ✦ J SPENCER ✦ G SPICE ✦ L SPICE ✦ D SPICKETT ✦ A SPILLER ✦ M SPINKS ✦ M SPITERI ✦ N SPOONER ✦ T SPOULDING ✦ A SPRATT ✦ J SPRIGGS ✦ M SPRINGFORD ✦ R SQUIRES ✦ L STACHINS ✦ N STACY ✦ P STAFSKI ✦ E STAMATE ✦ A STAMMERS ✦ G STANCIAUSKAS ✦

M STANCIU ✦ S STANCOMBE ✦ M STANCU ✦ A STANDRING ✦ C STANFIELD ✦ K STANLEY ✦ P STAPLES ✦ A STAPLETON ✦ M STAPLETON ✦ A STATII ✦ S STEBLIN ✦ A STEEL ✦ G STEEL ✦ B STEERE ✦ I STEFAN ✦ R STEFANCO ✦ M STEFANOU ✦ R STEINHAUSER ✦ M STEPHENS ✦ M STEUEKES ✦ M STEVEN ✦ A STEVENS ✦ B STEVENS ✦ W STEVENS ✦ B STEVENSON ✦ K STEWART ✦ W STILWELL ✦ A STIMBIRYS ✦ I STIRBLI ✦ N STITT ✦ B STOEV ✦ C STOICA ✦ I STOICA ✦ I STOITSEV ✦ J STOKES ✦ K STOKES ✦ R STOKES ✦ B STORAR ✦ G STORER ✦ R STORER ✦ T STORER ✦ B STOREY ✦ T STOREY ✦ N STORRY ✦ J STORY ✦ G STOTEN ✦ S STOYANOV ✦ M STRATFORD ✦ C STRATULAT ✦ G STRINGER ✦ F STROE ✦ D STROKAS ✦ D STRONACH ✦ B STRUTTOW ✦ P STRZYZEWSKI ✦ D STUPPLE ✦ D STYLIANIDES ✦ S STYLIANOU ✦ S STYLIANOU ✦ L SUAREZ ✦ M SUGDEN ✦ S SUHAREANU ✦ P SUKHU ✦ D SULLIVAN ✦ D SULLIVAN ✦ K SULLIVAN ✦ M SULLIVAN ✦ P SULLIVAN ✦ R SUMINSKAS ✦ V SURGAUTAS ✦ M SUSTR ✦ M SUTHERLAND ✦ V SUTTON ✦ C SVENSON ✦ M SWABY ✦ C SWAIN ✦ M SWALES ✦ D SWANN ✦ J SWEENEY ✦ A SWIDERSKA ✦ J SWINBOURNE ✦ G SYKES ✦ E SYLVA ✦ M SYMMONDS ✦ M SYULEYMAN ✦ K SZCZEPANSKI ✦ T SZCZYEIEL ✦ R SZCZYRSKI ✦ A SZENES ✦ B SZILARD ✦ B SZLAJBER ✦ M SZLAZAK ✦ P SZLAZAK ✦ M SZMANDA ✦ D SZMULEWICZ ✦ S TAAFFEE ✦ G TABRAM ✦ P TABUS ✦ S TAFT ✦ I TAGGART ✦ R TAIWO ✦ E TALKEVICIUS ✦ D TAMAS ✦ R TANASE ✦ V TANEH ✦ D TAPLIN ✦ A TARAKEVICIUS ✦ I TARAN ✦ R TARNOVAN ✦ R TASHKOV ✦ F TATE ✦ R TATE ✦ B TATTAN ✦ A TAYLOR ✦ A TAYLOR ✦ A TAYLOR ✦ D TAYLOR ✦ D TAYLOR ✦ H TAYLOR ✦ I TAYLOR ✦ J TAYLOR ✦ J TAYLOR ✦ L TAYLOR ✦ M TAYLOR ✦ M TAYLOR ✦ P TAYLOR ✦ P TAYLOR ✦ P TAYLOR ✦ R TAYLOR ✦ R TAYLOR-PRESSLAND ✦ T TAYLORE ✦ J TEAGLE ✦ L TEAGL ✦ K TEALE ✦ D TEARALL ✦ L TEER ✦ S TEGZES ✦ S TEMPLE ✦ D TENENIS ✦ M TENENIS ✦ G TENNANT ✦ H TERZIA ✦ R TERZIYSKI ✦ F TEUMA ✦ S THEOBALD ✦ A THOMAS C THOMAS ✦ J THOMAS ✦ L THOMAS ✦ M THOMAS ✦ M THOMAS ✦ N THOMAS ✦ R THOMAS ✦ S THOMAS ✦ A THOMPSON ✦ D THOMPSON ✦ D THOMPSON ✦ D THOMPSON ✦ D THOMPSON ✦ J THOMPSON ✦ J THOMPSON ✦ J THOMPSON ✦ K THOMPSON ✦ M THOMPSON ✦ M THOMPSON ✦ N THOMPSON ✦ P THOMPSON ✦ R THOMPSON ✦ S THOMPSON ✦ M THOMS ✦ D THOMSON ✦ M THOMSON ✦ P THOMSON ✦ C THORMAN ✦ T THORNBURROW ✦ J THORNE ✦ A THORNE-CLARKE ✦ R THORNTON ✦ A TIBBS ✦ R TIBERIU ✦ I TIGVA ✦ V TIHON ✦ F TILCIU ✦ M TILEY ✦ S TILL ✦ S TIMMS ✦ O TIMOTHY ✦ D TIRNOVEANU ✦ V TIRON ✦ S TITHERIDGE ✦ I TITIENI ✦ P TITOV ✦ M TKACZ ✦ M TOBIN ✦ P TOCHER ✦ E TODOROV ✦ S TODOROV ✦ D TOMELTY ✦ A TOMKINSON ✦ C TOMLIN ✦ A TOMLINSON ✦ J TOMLINSON ✦ G TONGE ✦ M TONKIN ✦ T TOOMEY ✦ A TOORE ✦ J TORKARSKI ✦ S TORKARSKI ✦ J TORR ✦ S TOTTEN ✦ C TOV ✦ D TOVEY ✦ J TOWNROW ✦ J TOWNSEND ✦ L TRAN ✦ P TREANOR ✦ D TRICKER ✦ A TRILL ✦ K TROCHA ✦ E TROFIMIUK ✦ A TROTMAN ✦ R TROTMAN ✦ Q TRUNI ✦ R TRUSS ✦ M TRYGUBETS ✦ L TRYLES ✦ G TSENOV ✦ G TSONEV ✦ E TUDOR ✦ C TUDOSE ✦ M TUERENA ✦ D TULLY ✦ S TUNGATE ✦ S TUPPIN ✦ D TURDEAN ✦ A TURNBULL ✦ P TURNBULL ✦ G TURNER ✦ J TURNER ✦ J TURNER ✦ L TURNER ✦ N TURNER ✦ V TURNER ✦ J TURNOCK ✦ K TURNOCK ✦ R TURTON ✦ I TUVEY ✦ J TWOMEY ✦ D TWUM-BARIMA ✦ G TWYMAN ✦ O TYE ✦ K TYLER ✦ M TYRELL ✦ D TYRRELL ✦ H UGBAJA ✦ B UMPLEBY ✦ A UNGUREANU ✦ C UNGUREANU ✦ P UNTERFRANC ✦ K URBANOWICZ ✦ S URHIOFE ✦ A URID ✦ D USHER ✦ I USSEF ✦ V UTYRA ✦ K UYIGUE ✦ D UYS ✦ C UZOMA ✦ G VADANA ✦ M VADANDU ✦ M VADUKUL ✦ A VAIVUTSKAS ✦ K VAKLINOV ✦ J VALENTE ✦ S VALENTIN ✦ B VALERIU ✦ V VALKANOV ✦ V VALKAUSKAS ✦ V VALKOV ✦ J VAN GENT ✦ K VAN MALDER ✦ E VAN VEEN ✦ A VARBACHEV ✦ D VARNAS ✦ Z VARNAUSKAS ✦ M VASILE ✦ R VASILERJSKIJ ✦ S VASILEV ✦ V VASILEV ✦ I VASILIAUSKAS ✦ A VASKYS ✦ M VAUGHAN ✦ N VEKARIA ✦ S VELICHKOV ✦ G VELIKOV ✦ L VENETTCO ✦ A VERLING ✦ S VEZBAUICIUS ✦ J VEZELIS ✦ M VIDAL ✦ I VIERU ✦ D VIGILANTE ✦ E VIITA ✦ M VILKINIS ✦ T VILLAS ✦ J VIRGINIJUS ✦ S VIRJILIO ✦ S VIRRUTIS ✦ N VISILEU ✦ S VISILIAN ✦ C VLAD ✦ B VLAHOV ✦ I VOICU ✦ P VOICU ✦ C VUC ✦ I VURAULE ✦ T WAGNER ✦ L WAITE ✦ M WAITE ✦ T WAITE ✦ B WAKEFIELD ✦ D WAKELIN ✦ T WAKELIN ✦ S WALE ✦ R WALGROVE ✦ M WALISZEWSKI ✦ A WALKER ✦ M WALKER ✦ M WALKER ✦ R WALKER ✦ A WALL ✦ C WALL ✦ S WALLER ✦ S WALLER ✦ P WALLIS ✦ E WALSH ✦ P WALSH ✦ P WALSH ✦ S WALSH ✦ D WALTERS ✦ D WALTON ✦ S WARBURTON ✦ M WARD ✦ M WARD ✦ P WARD ✦ T WAREING ✦ M WARHAM ✦ G WARREN ✦ J WARREN ✦ J WARREN ✦ C WARRENER ✦ L WASHINGTON ✦ A WATERMAN ✦ K WATERMAN ✦ S WATERS ✦ T WATKINS ✦ I WATSON ✦ G WATSON ✦ G WATSON ✦ J WATSON ✦ J WATSON ✦ P WATSON ✦ T WATSON ✦ D WATTERS ✦ I WATTERSON ✦ B WAYGOOD ✦ M WAZNY ✦ M WEAIT ✦ A WEALANDS ✦ S WEATHERALL ✦ D WEBB ✦ D WEBB ✦ D WEBB ✦ G WEBB ✦ J WEBB ✦ R WEBB ✦ S WEBB ✦ S WEBB-BOWEN ✦ T WEBBEL ✦ K WEBSTER ✦ R WEE ✦ R WEEKES ✦ G WEEKS ✦ R WEEKS ✦ A WELCH ✦ D WELCH ✦ R WELCH ✦ S WELDON ✦ S WELLINGS ✦ A WELLS ✦ A WELLS ✦ M WELTER ✦ S WELTER ✦ T WERIVER ✦ G WEST ✦ K WEST ✦ J WESTERBERG ✦ B WESTON ✦ A WESTWOOD ✦ D WESTWOOD ✦ J WHALEY ✦ N WHANTON ✦ B WHEELER ✦ A WHITE ✦ A WHITE ✦ J WHITE ✦ J WHITE ✦ N WHITE ✦ N WHITE ✦ R WHITE ✦ S WHITE ✦ G WHITEHEAD ✦ M WHITEHEAD ✦ V WHITEHEAD ✦ M WHITELEY ✦ J WHITEWOOD ✦ R WHITMEE ✦ G WHITTAKER ✦ P WICKS ✦ A WIELOGORSEI ✦ A WILD ✦ D WILKINS ✦ J WILL ✦ L WILLIAM ✦ A WILLIAMS ✦ A WILLIAMS ✦ C WILLIAMS ✦ C WILLIAMS ✦ G WILLIAMS ✦ J WILLIAMS ✦ J WILLIAMS ✦ J WILLIAMS ✦ K WILLIAMS ✦ K WILLIAMS ✦ K WILLIAMS ✦ L WILLIAMS ✦ M WILLIAMS ✦ N WILLIAMS ✦ T WILLIAMS ✦ S WILLIAMS ✦ D WILLIAMSON ✦ M WILLIAMSON ✦ A WILLIS ✦ M WILLIS ✦ R WILLIS ✦ S WILLIS ✦ T WILLIS ✦ P WILLISON ✦ A WILLS ✦ C WILSON ✦ C WILSON ✦ D WILSON ✦ G WILSON ✦ J WILSON ✦ L WILSON ✦ M WILSON ✦ M WILSON ✦ M WILSON ✦ O WILSON ✦ R WILSON ✦ M WILTSHIRE ✦ K WINIARCZYK ✦ A WINTER ✦ C WINTER ✦ N WISE ✦ B WITASZEK ✦ P WITKOWSKI ✦ M WITOWSKI ✦ D WITTON ✦ R WNEK ✦ R WOJCIK ✦ R WOJSZWILLO ✦ D WOJTKOWSKI ✦ T WOLODZKO ✦ R WOMBILL ✦ C WOOD ✦ D WOOD ✦ N WOOD ✦ P WOOD ✦ M WOODGATE ✦ B WOODHEAD ✦ L WOODHEAD ✦ D WOODHOUSE ✦ A WOODLEY ✦ D WOODS ✦ R WOODS ✦ G WOOLARD ✦ C WOOLCOTT ✦ J WOOLER ✦ G WOOLFORD ✦ B WOOLLEY ✦ M WOOLLSCROFT ✦ C WOOTEN ✦ J WORKMAN ✦ J WORMAN ✦ Z WOZNIAK ✦ P WRAY ✦ A WRIGHT ✦ K WRIGHT ✦ P WRIGHT ✦ P WRIGHT ✦ T WRIGHT ✦ W WRIGHT ✦ W WRIGHT ✦ T WRONSKI ✦ B WRZAL ✦ B WYATT ✦ A WYDERSKI ✦ L WYLDE ✦ D XHEVDEI ✦ A YANEV ✦ S YAPAR ✦ S YARDLEY ✦ C YARIAN ✦ P YATES ✦ E YELENCHAK ✦ V YEVTEICHIEVICH ✦ P YORDANOU ✦ A YORDANOV ✦ G YORDANOV ✦ I YORDANOV ✦ D YOSEF ✦ M YOUENS ✦ F YOUNG ✦ M YOUNG ✦ S YOUNG ✦ T YOUNG ✦ M YOUSSOUF ✦ G YOZOV ✦ V ZABIELA ✦ I ZAGHLOUL ✦ I ZAIKOVS ✦ P ZAJECKI ✦ D ZAKRZEWSKI ✦ K ZALA ✦ M ZAMMIT ✦ R ZAVORONKOV ✦ G ZAWADZK ✦ M ZAWADZKI ✦ M ZAWADZKI ✦ D ZBOROWSKI ✦ S ZEBRAUSKAS ✦ B ZENOV ✦ Z ZHELEV ✦ Z ZHELEV ✦ V ZHELYAZKOV ✦ T ZHIVKO ✦ M ZIENKIEWICZ ✦ J ZIEWIECKI ✦ S ZIMBA ✦ D ZLATCU ✦ T ZOCHOWSKI ✦ D ZONDWAYO ✦ S ZULU ✦ M ZYMERI

LIST OF WORKS

The Winter Garden

Now known as the Beaufort Bar, the Winter Garden was once an annexe to the adjacent Thames Foyer, providing an alternative dining and entertainment venue for Edwardian society. A glass ceiling would open in the summer, while in the winter artificial roses twined around the walls and chandeliers brought colour to grey London days. By the mid-1920s, when bright young things tangoed their way across the Thames Foyer, the Winter Garden was remodelled. The epitome of a chic nightclub, it had a stage for the Savoy Bands, and the famous 'rising floor', which rose three feet on hydraulic lifts to allow good views of the cabaret acts that performed there.

Semi-Secret Vantage Point

The Upper Thames Foyer has always been the 'crossroads' of The Savoy. From a pretty, curved bay window with an ornate plaster lattice, set high in one corner of the room, the curious could watch hotel guests and visitors rushing through the foyer on their way to somewhere else. As part of the restoration project, this semi-secret vantage point was replicated in mirror image in the opposite corner of the Upper Thames Foyer, allowing a second view of the hustle and bustle below. These paired windows sit above the two curved bays of the new Savoy Tea, whose Georgian-inspired frontage allows glimpses of the treasures within.

River View Guestrooms

As originally built in 1889, The Savoy guestrooms were located on the second to sixth floors, with a seventh floor offering accommodation for guests' servants. By 1910 it was clear that more guestrooms were needed, as well as additional bathrooms, despite a then-unheard-of ratio of one bathroom for every three guestrooms. As a result, an enormous building project began to extend the hotel's river-front forward, creating space for additional bathrooms, and adding two floors to the hotel on the Thames side. The original Victorian guest rooms were redecorated in Edwardian style to match the rooms on the new floors. In later decades the eighth floor would again be remodelled, in the latest Art Deco style.

Natural Light

When the Thames Foyer was originally built in 1904, a series of large skylights around the edge of the ceiling allowed natural light into the room. These were hastily boarded up when blackout regulations came into force at the beginning of World War II; the windows posed an additional risk to morale, as they reminded guests that there was nothing above this ceiling but sky and a direct hit could have proved lethal. Happily, The Savoy survived the Blitz almost unscathed, but the windows never gained a reprieve and were finally lost during the 1960s' redecoration of the Thames Foyer. The 2010 restoration project provided an excellent excuse to bring natural light back to this room.

City Illuminations

The Savoy's Embankment location overlooking the Thames, with wonderful views of Cleopatra's Needle and the Houses of Parliament, is unrivalled among London hotels. Richard D'Oyly Carte was lucky to acquire a plot of land facing Embankment Gardens, just south of the Savoy Theatre, and clever enough to realize the potential of the view by designing his new hotel with wide balconies that ran all along the riverfront. Although the balconies are long gone, the 2010 restoration has allowed the architects to ensure that windows on the river side maximise the iconic Thames views. D'Oyly Carte's vision has been supplemented by the magnificent view at night-time when the city is illuminated.

A Royal Event

The Thames Foyer is rarely given over to private events, but a notable exception was made on the evening of the Queen's Coronation in 1953 when every public room in the hotel was reserved for The Savoy's own Coronation Ball. Many of the guests at the ball had also attended the Coronation ceremony earlier in the day and came to the evening event resplendent in their Coronation attire and jewels. The Thames Foyer was turned into a huge Tudor-style tent to reflect the new Elizabethan age. There was an enormous canopy of pleated fabric, ostrich plumes and heraldic decorations on the pillars, small ornamental box hedges and even Beefeaters, hired for the evening.

Former Glory

The Savoy was arranged around the four sides of a central courtyard. When the Strand entrance to the hotel was constructed in 1904, this courtyard was no longer in daily use. In 1905, the entire courtyard was sealed and flooded in imitation of a Venetian canal for the famous Gondola Party thrown by American millionaire George Kessler. In part, this influenced the desire to create a larger banqueting space than the hotel already possessed. The Lancaster Ballroom was built into the old courtyard and modelled on an 18th century French salon. It remains almost entirely as it would have appeared on the day of its first ever event: a US Naval Ball, which took place in December 1910.

A Jewel in the Crown

This luxurious suite, encompassing eight of the rooms on the river side of the fifth floor, offers a rare chance to live like a king, or even a maharajah. The Maharajah of Patiala habitually took all these rooms as one single suite for himself and his family when they came to London for the summer in the 1920s. Hollywood 'royalty' also enjoyed lengthy sojourns here, and the Impressionist artist Claude Monet painted some of his stunning watercolours from these windows when his sixth-floor suite was unavailable. Monet stayed for months at a time, and returned to The Savoy in subsequent years to continue his series of paintings of London's bridges and the Houses of Parliament.

An Artist's Eye View

This beautifully restored River View Suite offers unparalleled views of the Thames from its wide windows. On a clear day, seven bridges are visible from this suite. The distinctive view has always attracted artists, the first being James McNeill Whistler, a great friend of Richard D'Oyly Carte. He sketched the scaffolding surrounding the hotel as it was being built, and later moved into a sixth-floor suite with his dying wife in order to make her last days as comfortable as possible and to distract himself by sketching views from this high vantage point. This possibly inspired future artists to take advantage of this unique elevated view of the River Thames.

Gilded Elegance

Newly created during the 2010 restoration to complement The Savoy's legendary American Bar, the Beaufort Bar was installed on the historic stage where the Savoy Bands played nightly and stars, from Noël Coward to Josephine Baker, entertained diners from the 1920s until the 1980s. The Lalique-style illuminated glass bar stands centre stage, while the gilded alcoves around the room reflect light from the elegant Murano chandelier. The sophisticated Art Deco décor and theatrical bar setting bring a 21st-century twist to this elegant room, which was named after the family of John of Gaunt, Duke of Lancaster, an early inhabitant of the original Savoy Palace after which the hotel is named.

Savoy external lettering
in Savoy Grill
June 2009

5th Floor River Suite 516
December 2007

5th Floor River Suite 515
December 2007

5th Floor River Suite 514
December 2007

5th Floor Monet Suite 513
December 2007

5th Floor Monet Suite 512
December 2007

5th Floor Monet Suite 511
December 2007

5th Floor River Suite 510
December 2007

5th Floor River Suite 509
December 2007

5th Floor River Suite 508
December 2007

American Bar
February 2008

Reception
February 2008

Edwardian Suite
March 2008

Edwardian Guestroom
March 2008

Art Deco Suite
June 2008

Beaufort Bar
April 2009

River Suite 314
March 2008

Monet Suite 513
March 2008

Edwardian Guestroom 355
June 2008

Princess IDA Room
March 2008

Pinafore Room
March 2008

Reception
April 2009

Guestroom 852
May 2008

River Room 812
April 2009

Art Deco Room
May 2008

Guest Suite 958
bedroom
May 2008

Basement
December 2008

Guest Suite 958
bathroom
May 2008

American Bar
original wallpaper
September 2008

5th Floor River View Suite
river view
May 2008

Pinafore Lobby
stair
March 2008

Entrance Lobby
view towards Thames Foyer
March 2008

Entrance Lobby
fireplace
February 2008

Records Store
March 2008

5th Floor River View Suite 516
December 2008

5th Floor River View Suite 515
December 2008

5th Floor River View Suite 514
December 2008

5th Floor Monet Suite 513
December 2008

5th Floor Monet Suite 512
December 2008

5th Floor Monet Suite 511
December 2008

5th Floor River View Suite 510
December 2008

5th Floor River View Suite 509
December 2008

5th Floor River View Suite 508
December 2008

River View Suites 716 / 715
April 2009

Princess IDA Room
October 2008

Entrance to American Bar
May 2009

Guestroom
July 2011

Entrance Lobby
April 2009

Upper Thames Foyer
new vantage point
September 2009

Upper Thames Foyer
May 2009

Upper Thames Foyer
old vantage point
September 2009

River Restaurant
May 2009

River Restaurant
March 2010

Royal Suite
February 2010

Guestroom 428
July 2009

Corridor
June 2009

Thames Foyer
December 2009

Thames Foyer
December 2009

Entrance Lobby
August 2009

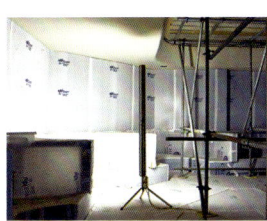

Savoy Grill
June 2009

Entrance to American Bar
August 2009

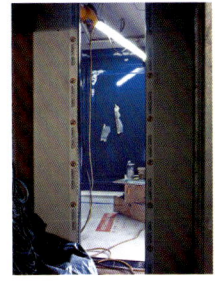

Blue Lift
April 2010

Royal Suite
river view
January 2010

Scaffolding
June 2008

5th Floor Royal Suite
bedroom
August 2009

5th Floor Royal Suite
dressing room
August 2009

5th Floor Royal Suite
bathroom
August 2009

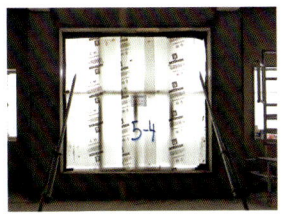

5th Floor Royal Suite
dining room
August 2009

5th Floor Royal Suite
sitting room
August 2009

5th Floor Royal Suite
office
August 2009

5th Floor Royal Suite
guestroom
August 2009

5th Floor Royal Suite,
guestroom en suite
August 2009

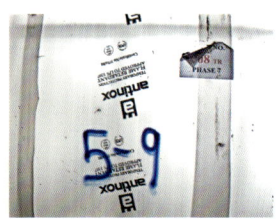

5th Floor River View Suite 514
August 2009

Royal Suite
sitting room
May 2010

Royal Suite
master bedroom
May 2010

Royal Suite
silk-wrapped chandelier
July 2010

Royal Suite
office
January 2010

Thames Foyer
April 2010

Reception
August 2010

Reception
August 2010

Gondoliers Room
August 2010

Gondoliers Room
August 2010

Entrance Lobby
fireplace
March 2010

Royal Suite
office
August 2010

Royal Suite
sitting room
August 2010

7th Floor River View
May 2010

7th Floor River Suite
July 2010

7th Floor River Suite
bathroom
July 2010

Art Deco Guest Suite 958
bedroom
June 2009

Art Deco Guest Suite 958
bedroom
June 2009

Art Deco Guest Suite 958
bathroom
December 2009

Art Deco Guest Suite 958
sitting room
April 2010

American Bar
August 2010

American Bar
October 2011

5th Floor Royal Suite
master bedroom
July 2011

5th Floor Royal Suite
dressing room
July 2011

5th Floor Royal Suite
bathroom
July 2011

5th Floor Royal Suite
dining room
July 2011

5th Floor Royal Suite
sitting room
July 2011

5th Floor Royal Suite
office
July 2011

5th Floor Royal Suite
guestroom
July 2011

5th Floor Royal Suite
guestroom en suite
July 2011

5th Floor River View Suite 514
July 2011

5th Floor Royal Suite
lobby
November 2010

5th Floor Royal Suite
office
November 2010

5th Floor Royal Suite
river view
November 2010

5th Floor Royal Suite
sitting room
October 2010

5th Floor Royal Suite
painting
October 2010

5th Floor Royal Suite
dining room
November 2010

5th Floor Royal Suite
master bedroom
November 2010

5th Floor Royal Suite
master bedroom
November 2010

Lancaster Ballroom
September 2010

Upper Thames Foyer
October 2010

Upper Thames Foyer
September 2010

Upper Thames Foyer
October 2010

Thames Foyer
October 2010

Entrance Lobby
October 2010

Entrance Lobby
September 2010

River Restaurant
October 2010

River Restaurant
October 2010

Katharine Hepburn Suite
September 2010

Beaufort Bar
October 2010

River Restaurant
private dining
October 2010

Savoy Grill
November 2010

Boodles Boutique
July 2011

Royal Suite
September 2010

A warm thank you to the following people, without whom this book would not have been possible.

To the staff at The Savoy for all their assistance; to the management for supporting this project to the very end – in particular Kiaran Macdonald, Julian Haddon and Brett Perkins.

To Chris Cahill – Fairmont Hotels & Resorts, Patsy Byrne – Byrne Group plc and Tony Plato – Chorus Group for their support in publishing this book.

To the Chorus staff for their assistance and good humour, which made my working days on site a lot more enjoyable.

To my assistants, Julia Glover, Daniella Fleckenstein and Jonathan Anrep on capturing the 5th Floor River View Suites – the only photographs that required lighting.

I am indebted to Rachael Connolly for introducing me to The Savoy.

To Paula Hickey for her huge support and attention to detail.

To David Gibbs, Ian McDonald and Kate Pope for assistance on the text.

To Susan Scott for her research, Savoy knowledge and then getting it down on paper.

Gavin Jack for his invaluable editing insight.

Dewi Lewis for publishing.

Andy Ford and Klair Bird at Spectrum Photographic.

To Atul for his endless amount of good advice, encouragement and complete support.

First Edition 2011
Published by Dewi Lewis Publishing

Book Design by ph design
Edited by Siobhán Doran and Paula Hickey
Texts by HRH Prince Alwaleed Bin Talal Bin Abdulaziz Alsaud,
Chris Cahill, David Gibbs, Siobhán Doran, Susan Scott
and Patsy Byrne

Photographs by Siobhán Doran
Photograph, page 5 courtesy of The Savoy

Print by EBS, Verona, Italy

ISBN: 978-1-907893-14-8

Dewi Lewis Publishing
8 Broomfield Road
Heaton Moor
Stockport Sk4 4ND
England
www.dewilewispublishing.com